PHILIP PULLMAN

Philip Pullman was born in Norwich, England in 1946 and grew up in Zimbabwe and Wales. He worked as a teacher for many years and his first children's novel, *Count Karlstein*, came out in 1982. *The Ruby in the Smoke*, the first of the Sally Lockhart quartet of Victorian thrillers, was published in 1985.

He has won many awards for his children's books, including the Carnegie Medal, the *Guardian* Children's Book Award, the Smarties Prize, the Astrid Lindgren Memorial Award, the Whitbread Book of the Year Award and a CBE. His acclaimed fantasy trilogy, *His Dark Materials* (Scholastic Books in the UK and Knopf in the US), comprising *Northern Lights*, *The Subtle Knife* and *The Amber Spyglass*, has been published in thirty-nine languages, and even in graphic novel form (with the French publishers, Gallimard). The first volume is now a major motion picture, released in 2007. The BBC, in line with Bad Wolf Productions, have recently commissioned a new drama series based on *His Dark Materials*, on which Philip is to be an executive producer.

Philip's other books for children and young adults include *Clockwork, I Was a Rat!*, and *The New Cut Gang* books; *Thunderbolt's Waxwork* and *The Gas-Fitter's Ball*. *Once Upon a Time in the North* was published in April 2008. He is working on *The Book of Dust*, another book about the characters in the *His Dark Materials* trilogy.

In 2010 Philip published his controversial number-one bestseller *The Good Man Jesus and the Scoundrel Christ*.

Philip Pullman lives in Oxford with his wife, and has two sons.

PHILIP WILSON

Philip Wilson is a director, whose recent credits include *Beacons* (Park Theatre); *The Three Lions* (St. James Theatre/Edinburgh/ UK tour); *How Many Miles to Babylon?* (Lyric Belfast); *Toro! Toro!* (national tour); *Twist of Gold* (Polka); *The Norman Conquests*, *Noises Off*, *Dr Faustus* and *The Astonished Heart/ Still Life* (Liverpool Playhouse); the books of Ruth and 2 Samuel in *Sixty-Six Books* (Bush Theatre/Westminster Abbey); *The Importance of Being Earnest/Travesties* (Birmingham Rep); *If Love Were All* and *In Praise of Love* (Minerva, Chichester); *The Found Man* (Traverse); *Un Uomo Trovato* (Teatro della Limonaia, Florence); *Ain't Misbehavin'* (Sheffield Crucible) and *Breaking the Code* (Theatre Royal, Northampton).

He is the former Artistic Director of Salisbury Playhouse (2007–11), where he directed *The Game of Love and Chance*, *The Constant Wife*, *The Picture*, *Private Lives*, *Arsenic and Old Lace*, *The Winslow Boy*, his own adaptation of JL Carr's *A Month in the Country*, *What the Butler Saw*, *People at Sea*, *Alphabetical Order* and *Corpse!* He also directed and designed *Blackbird*, *Faith Healer* and *Toro! Toro!* (TMA Award nomination, Best Show for Children and Young People).

Philip spent two years as a producer for the BBC, and was the Performance Consultant for the film *Shakespeare in Love*. He won the Regional Theatre Young Director Scheme bursary in 1995, and in 2015 was awarded the David Fraser/Andrea Wonfor Directing for Television Bursary.

His book, *Dramatic Adventures in Rhetoric*, written with Giles Taylor, is published by Oberon Books.

Philip Pullman's

GRIMM TALES
for Young and Old

adapted for the stage by
Philip Wilson

NICK HERN BOOKS
London
www.nickhernbooks.co.uk

A Nick Hern Book

Philip Pullman's Grimm Tales for Young and Old first published in this dramatised version in Great Britain in 2016 as a paperback original by Nick Hern Books Limited, The Glasshouse, 49a Goldhawk Road, London W12 8QP

All Tales copyright © 2012 Philip Pullman
Adaptation copyright © 2016 Philip Wilson

Philip Pullman and Philip Wilson have asserted their moral right to be identified as the authors of this work

Cover image: Richard Davenport

Designed and typeset by Nick Hern Books, London
Printed in the UK by CPI Books (UK) Ltd

A CIP catalogue record for this book is available from the British Library

ISBN 978 1 84842 508 8

With thanks to everyone who was involved with the two productions, at Shoreditch Town Hall and at Bargehouse.

This script is a testament to their imagination, invention, creativity – and hard work.

Contents

This volume contains dramatisations of twelve different Tales arranged in two complementary groups – enough material for two complete productions. Alternatively, companies can make their own selection as required, with the fees reflecting the number of Tales to be told.

Foreword
Philip Pullman

When Penguin Classics asked me if I was interested in writing a fresh version of some of the tales of the Brothers Grimm, I had to suppress a whoop of delight. Actually, I'm not sure that I did suppress it. I've always relished folk tales, and the famous Grimm collection is one of the richest of all. It was a dream of a job.

Reading them through carefully and making notes, I was struck again by the freshness, the swiftness, the sheer strangeness of the best of them. I was being asked to choose fifty or so out of the more than two hundred, and there were certainly at least that many that deserved a new outing. The most interesting thing, perhaps, from a dramatic point of view, is that they consist entirely of events: there's no character development, because the characters are not fully developed three-dimensional human beings so much as fixed, flat types like those of the *commedia dell'arte*, or like the little cardboard actors (a penny plain, tuppence-coloured) we find in the toy theatre. If we're looking for psychological depth, we won't find it in the fairy tale.

Nor is there anything in the way of poetic description or rich and musical language. Princesses are beautiful, forests are dark, witches are wicked, things are as red as blood or as white as snow: it's all very perfunctory.

What we find instead of these literary qualities is a wonderful freedom and zest, entirely unencumbered by likelihood. The most marvellous or preposterous or hilarious or terrifying events happen with all the swiftness of dreams. They work splendidly for oral telling, and the very best of them have a quality that C.S. Lewis ascribed to myths: we remember them instantly after only one hearing, and we never forget them. The job of anyone telling them again is to do so as clearly as possible, and not let their own personality get in the way.

They can be told, of course, and they can be dramatised, in any
of a thousand different ways. They have been many times, and
they will be many more. This particular version was very
enjoyable for me to read and to watch because Philip Wilson is
so faithful to the clarity and the force of the events, just as
Jacob and Wilhelm Grimm were faithful to the talents of the
various storytellers whose words they listened to and
transcribed two hundred years ago. And they still work.

Telling Tales
Philip Wilson

The Brothers Grimm's stories have been retold countless times over the past two centuries. Katharine Mary Briggs, Italo Calvino and Marina Warner included versions in their classic collections of fairy tales, and writers such as Angela Carter, Terry Pratchett and Carol Ann Duffy have revelled in inventive variations. In recent years, two films of *Snow White* appeared, *Maleficent* re-imagined the story of Sleeping Beauty, Sondheim's *Into the Woods* was filmed, and Terry Gilliam gave the lives of the brothers themselves a high-spirited storybook twist in *The Brothers Grimm*. Moreover, the latest anthropological research indicates that the origins of folk tales such as *Little Red Riding Hood* and *Beauty and the Beast* can be traced back millennia.

In 2012, Philip Pullman selected fifty of his favourite Grimm Tales to retell. His intention in doing this, he declared, was 'to produce a version that was as clear as water'. In the same way, my dramatisations seek to retain the limpid and beautifully crafted character of the original stories. The telling of the Tales is shared between an ensemble of performers, who play husbands and wives, brothers and sisters, princes and princesses, wise kings and wicked witches, snakes and birds. The original productions, drawing on puppetry, movement and music, were a theatrical celebration of live storytelling. At Shoreditch Town Hall, we brought to life the adventures of *Little Red Riding Hood*, *Rapunzel*, *The Three Snake Leaves*, *Hans-my-Hedgehog* and *The Juniper Tree*. At Bargehouse, meanwhile, we retold the Tales of *The Frog King, or Iron Heinrich*, *The Three Little Men in the Woods*, *Thousandfurs*, *The Goose Girl at the Spring*, *Hansel and Gretel* and *Faithful Johannes*. Also included here is my adaptation of *The Donkey Cabbage*, a story we didn't find a home for, but is too good to forgo.

This was a deliberately eclectic selection, which embraced a variety of classic story plots – quests and voyages, rags to riches and overcoming monsters – within the core genres of comedy, tragedy, romance... and, sometimes, surrealist farce! Their appeal lay also in how they have echoes of Shakespeare and Ancient Greek tragedy, incorporating as they do rites of passage, ghosts of fathers, animal transformations. And how they embody the themes of human life: births, marriages and deaths; sibling support (or rivalry); parental cruelty; the hardships of poverty; jealousy and desire.

While it is eminently possible to stage these stories in traditional theatre environments, ours was an immersive approach: the audience were divided into groups, and took different journeys through the various parts of the venue. After each Tale, this group was guided by the performers to another space. On their way, they glimpsed images evoking hints of other Tales untold, as they passed through rooms from which other characters seemed to have only just departed – leaving Cinderella's pile of lentils by an iron stove; Snow White's glass coffin, along with seven identical small beds; Rumpelstiltskin's spinning wheel in a shaft of light, in a room with straw on one side and a cloud of gold objects on the other. And so on...

The world of the play was 'scruffy salvage': an elemental world of rough-hewn wood, tarnished metal, unrefined cloth. The costumes were tattered, puppets were constructed from found objects, and everyday items were often used in place of the thing described. All were transfomed by the Storytellers' investment in them. Wooden scrubbing brushes were sewn onto a duffle coat for Hans-my-Hedgehog's prickly skin; thick rope stood in for Rapunzel's hair; an enamel coffee pot became a white duck. This approach both ensured that these dark Tales were not prettified, and gave a sense that the performers had drawn on what might lie around them, to supplement and enhance the storytelling. We invited the audience to complete the picture with their imagination.

There was no attempt either to set the stories in the age in which they were written down or to transpose them to a contemporary setting. Rather, they existed in a glorious miscellany of different styles, periods and cultures – anchored by the 'scruffy salvage' aesthetic – to echo the magpie-like origins of the Tales. Nor were we constrained to Europe. In *The Three Snake Leaves*, the number four is very important. In China, this is a symbol of unluckiness – which chimes with this Tale's more Eastern feel: it doesn't read like it's from a Northern European tradition. Similarly, the Princess of the Golden Roof seemed to have travelled as far as she does with Faithful Johannes. These stories know no borders.

Interwoven with the action at Shoreditch was music, sung live, and drawn from *Der Zupfgeigenhansl* – a collection of German folk songs compiled by the *Wandervögel* or 'wandering bird' movement, which celebrated journeys of discovery. At Bargehouse, there was also a quartet of actor-musicians in glorious felt headdresses of a donkey, a dog, a cat and a cockerel, echoing another group of Grimm characters, the Musicians of Bremen.

After the performance, further spaces were revealed for the audience to explore, filled with hanging ballgowns; rooms filled with curious items; walls of bizarre and macabre images...

But that is just one approach. There are as many ways to tell a story as there are stories themselves. You only have to look at how the Tales have been illustrated: a brief internet search will reveal endless depictions in different styles, to offer inspiration. A very brief list might include: Elenore Abbott, Angela Barrett, Edward Burne-Jones, Katharine Cameron, Walter Crane, George Cruikshank, Gustave Doré, Edmund Dulac, David Hockney, Franz Jüttner, Margaret Pocock, Evans Price, Arthur Rackham... In recent years, fairy tales have also been drawn upon by a range of artists, from Paula Rego to the fashion photographer Tim Walker.

If you wish to delve more into the psychology of this world, the Queen, as it were, of fairy tales is Marina Warner: and you will find her work – including *Once Upon a Time* and *From the Beast to the Blonde: On Fairy Tales and their Tellers* – overflowing with ideas. Other books we referred to included Bruno Bettelheim's *The Uses of Enchantment: The Meaning and Importance of Fairy Tales*, Katharine Mary Briggs' three-volume *Folk-Tales of Britain* and Sheldon Cashdan's *The Witch Must Die: The Hidden Meaning of Fairy Tales*.

Although the stories are uncluttered in language and spare in detail, nonetheless they resonate with all manner of human experience. Philip Pullman is right that on the page, the characters appear flat: these are archetypes, defined by their class, profession or role in society. In fairy tales, people are what they do. This does not mean, though, that there is no room for *dramatic* characterisation. The stories certainly include tension and conflict. And they deal with universal situations, in which the drama often springs from family ties: the characters could be us. So we can add our detail or psychology, through expression, gesture, nuance… all of which springs from the engine of fairy tales, which is desire.

In the modern world, the depiction of women in fairy tales is controversial. Admittedly, there *are* archetypal 'evil' female characters, many of whom, as Marina Warner comments, 'occupy the heart of the home' – the wicked mother, the queen, and the fabled stepmother. These are often the agents of potent and lethal spells. Plus, there are also women as images of perfection, such as the Princess of the Golden Roof in *Faithful Johannes* – a goddess on earth. And there is a fair bit of crying…

However, the female characters are also supremely resourceful. In *The Juniper Tree*, Marleenken buries her brother's bones – and thereby starts the process of retribution on their evil stepmother. It's Gretel that kills the witch, releases Hansel and suggests they cross the lake on the duck's back one by one. Thousandfurs is also extremely resilient – both in creating obstacles against her incestuously lustful father, and then in ensuring that she stays safe. And although The Man's Daughter in *The Three Little Men in the Woods* is resolutely kind and unshakeably generous, she also won't stay dead! And returns (spoiler alert) to ensure that her stepmother and stepsister get their comeuppance.

In German, fairy tales are known as *wonder* tales. This term encourages us to celebrate these fantastic characters and episodes in all their eccentric glory, from the picturesque to the grotesque, and from the magical to the mundane – free, above all, from the sanitisation and lavish naturalism of later versions, not least Disney films.

Fairy tales exist in a world of enchanted forests and stone castles, soaring towers and bottomless seas. Plus, the action moves lightly and speedily from location to location. So it is key not to get bogged down in place. While there is a need to create a setting, an environment, an arena for storytelling, remember the appeal made by the Chorus in Shakespeare's *Henry V*, 'Think, when we talk of horses, that you see them.'

That word, talk, reminds us that although the Tales were written down, shaped and curated by the Brothers Grimm, these stories emerged from oral traditions: they have always been intended to be spoken aloud. There is an innate human desire to gather together and listen to a storyteller, or to witness a group reenacting a tale. My approach has been to divide up the voices among a group of Storytellers. Each Tale starts with some variation on 'Once...' (the universally agreed way of starting a story), followed by a brief introduction to the key figures and situation – along with their voices. Thereafter, the words are shared in three modes of speech: dialogue, narration and 'thinking aloud'. Viewpoint and attitude is crucial throughout. Also, you'll note how characters move from retelling to r*eliving* events: the intention is always to ensure that the story is immediate, is happening right now – not comfortably in the past.

This immediacy is particularly important in the second mode of speech, narration. Often, characters comment on the action; even before they have been fully introduced into the story. For instance, in *The Frog King*, The King observes and comments on The Princess, while Faithful Heinrich – the character least familiar to us in this Tale – does the same for his master, until at last he is able to tell his story. Sometimes, the characters cannot be aware of what is going on at a particular moment, but as Storytellers, they know all, and help to advance the Tale. This occurs especially at moments of secrecy, magic or ritual: such as when the Servants describe Thousandfurs' transformation for the balls, or when The King and The Queen observe The Goose Girl's washing ritual. While they do not have a role as such at this point, their connection to the story is no less opinionated, active, defined. And since they won't be able to change costume, the distinction must be made through vocal tone, within the guise of their main character.

Throughout the Tales, whether on the edge of the action or in the middle of it, no Storyteller is apart from it. And each one must be mindful always of their audience. Hamlet says, 'We'll hear a play tomorrow' – and however vivid and sensuous a production you create, at its heart should always be the words, and a delight in language.

The punctuation of Philip Pullman's text has been retained, so that it is clear where a phrase relates to the one before, and also which parts are dialogue, which narration, and which thinking aloud: in order to suggest the rhythm and patterns of sharing these speeches. He compares storytelling to jazz, observing that, 'the substance of the tale is there already, just as the sequence of chords in a song is there ready for a jazz musician, and our task is to step from chord to chord, from event to event, with all the lightness and swing we can.' That sense of working in tandem with other players, while retaining an improvisatory quality, is key to staging these Tales. It's all about the ensemble.

When creating a company, consider carefully the doubling between the Tales. Giving each perfomer a variety of roles – a witch in one, a kind woman in another; a wise man at first, a foolish one later – not only gives actors a fruitful challenge: it also heightens the sense that it is not always clear how people really are when you first meet them. Even *within* stories, there is much scope for doubling and transformation (what was done in the original productions is indicated at the start of each set of Tales). And bear in mind the power of the numbers three and seven: trios, in particular, are the staple of fairy tales.

Although any number of these Tales can be told, and in any order, in the original productions more familiar stories were performed first, before the audience was led into darker, less-well-known territories: deeper into the forest.

Much of the action is indicated within the storytelling: rather than demonstrate this, the staging should elucidate what is described. The language is spare: there is, deliberately, little there – which allows for nimble movement, a deft negotiation of the sudden shifts in situation. Stage directions have been kept to a minimum: generally, the text is its own prompt book. Most importantly, these Tales live most when they are imbued with the imaginations of those who are telling them: so it is not only right but crucial that you find your own path through the text.

Whichever route you take, what's important is what happens next. Philip Pullman has observed that, 'Swiftness is a great virtue in the fairy tale. A good tale moves with a dreamlike speed from event to event, pausing only to say as much as is needed and no more.'

My intention has been to tell these Tales with a similar economy, clarity and passion.

The first performance of the *First Set of Tales* took place at Shoreditch Town Hall, London, on 14 March 2014.

THE STORYTELLERS
Ashley Alymann
Sabina Arthur
Rebecca Bainbridge
Annabel Betts
James Byng
Paul Clerkin
Lindsay Dukes
Simon Wegrzyn

THE STORYMAKERS

Director	Philip Wilson
Set and Costume Designer	Tom Rogers
Lighting Designer	Howard Hudson
Composer and Sound Designer	Richard Hammarton
Assistant Director	Sarah Butcher
Casting Director	Kay Magson CDG
Costume Supervisor	Alexandra Kharibian
Puppet Maker	Sinéad Sexton
Design Assistants	Anna Jones
	Nancy Nicholson
	Nefelie Sidiropoulou
Producer	Valerie Coward
Executive Producer	Cat Botibol
Production Managers	Timothy Peacock
and Stage Managers	Cecily Rabey
Stage Manager	Chris Tuffin
Assistant Stage Manager	Sinéad Sexton
Wardrobe Mistress	Nicole Graham
Electrician	Adam Mottley
Sound Technician	Mark Cunningham
Production Photographer	Tom Medwell
Rehearsal Photographer	Matt Hass

Special thanks to Nick Giles and all the team at Shoreditch Town Hall.

The first performance of the *Second Set of Tales* took place at Bargehouse, Oxo Tower Wharf, South Bank, London on 21 November 2014.

THE STORYTELLERS
Kate Adler
Sabina Arthur
James Byng
Paul Clerkin
Morag Cross
Amanda Gordon
Leda Hodgson
Richard Mark
Nessa Matthews
Anthony Ofoegbu
Maria Omakinwa
Joel Robinson
Megan Salter
John Seaward
Johnson Willis
Robert Willoughby

THE STORYMAKERS

Director	Philip Wilson
Set and Costume Designer	Tom Rogers
Lighting Designer	Howard Hudson
Composer and Sound Designer	Richard Hammarton
Assistant Director	Sarah Butcher
Magic Consultant	Darren Lang
Casting Director	Kay Magson CDG
Costume Supervisor	Jennie Falconer
Puppet Designer and Maker	Alison Duddle
Animal Headdress Maker	Barbara Keal
Design Assistants	Robson Barreto
	Simon Bejer
	Mika Handley
	Nefelie Sidiropoulou
Instrument Design	Flora Pickering

Producer	Valerie Coward
Executive Producer	Cat Botibol
Production Manager	Andy Reader
Stage Manager and Assistant Production Manager	Timothy Peacock
Technical Stage Manager	William Cottrell
Deputy Stage Manager	Ellen Dawson
Assistant Stage Managers	Kirsty MacDiarmid
	Sinéad Sexton
	Alice Barber
Wardrobe Mistresses	Lydia Cawson
	Nicole Graham
Master Carpenter	Dario Fusco
Carpenters	Stuart Farnell
	Ben Lee
	Rob Pearce
	Ben Porter
	Bob Weatherhead
Set Build Assistants	Henry Culpepper
	Natalie Favaloro
	Sasha Mani
Scenic Coordinator	Georgina Foster
Scenic Art	Ashleigh Blair
	Bethe Crews
	Charlotte Lane
Chief Electrician	Laurence Russell
Deputy Chief Electrician	Jordan Lightfoot
Lighting Technicians	Sarah Harrison
	Scott Hislop
	Ben Redding
Production Sound	Mike Walker
	Chris Simpson
	Ryan Griffin
	for Loh-Humm Audio
Front of House Manager	Chris Burkitt
Design Director	Gareth Paul Jones
Copywriter	Josephine Ring
Web Development	Merlin Mason
Assistant to Producers	Nadia Aminzadeh

Production Photographer   Matt Hass
Rehearsal Photographer   Tom Medwell

Special thanks to all the team at Bargehouse.

'All we need is the word "Once…"
and we're off'

Philip Pullman

THE FIRST SET OF TALES

Little Red Riding Hood
Rapunzel
The Three Snake Leaves
Hans-my-Hedgehog
The Juniper Tree

The Storytellers

Little Red Riding Hood

LITTLE RED RIDING HOOD
THE MOTHER
THE WOLF
THE GRANDMOTHER
THE HUNTSMAN

This Tale can be told by a cast of four:
Little Red Riding Hood
The Mother / The Grandmother
The Wolf
The Huntsman

Rapunzel

THE WIFE
THE HUSBAND
THE WITCH
RAPUNZEL
THE PRINCE
RAPUNZEL'S SON
RAPUNZEL'S DAUGHTER

This Tale can be told by a cast of four:
The Wife / Rapunzel
The Husband / Rapunzel's Son (*puppet*)
The Witch / Rapunzel's Daughter (*puppet*)
The Prince

The Three Snake Leaves

THE POOR MAN
THE SON, *later* THE SOLDIER
THE KING
THE SECOND SOLDIER
THE THIRD SOLDIER
THE PRINCESS
A SENTRY
THE SOLDIER'S SERVANT
THE CAPTAIN

This Tale can be told by a cast of four:
The Poor Man / The Third Soldier / A Sentry /
    The Soldier's Servant
The Son, *later* The Soldier
The King / The Captain
The Princess / The Second Soldier

Hans-my-Hedgehog

HANS-MY-HEDGEHOG
THE FARMER
THE WIFE
THE MAIDSERVANT
THE FIRST FARMER
THE SECOND FARMER
THE PRIEST
THE FIRST KING
THE SERVANT
A COURTIER
THE FIRST PRINCESS
THE SECOND KING
THE MESSENGER
THE SECOND PRINCESS
A FARMER
ANOTHER FARMER
A THIRD FARMER
THE PHYSICIAN

This Tale can be told by a cast of four:
The Farmer / The Servant / The Second King / A Third Farmer
The Wife / A Courtier / The Messenger / The First Princess
    A Farmer / The Physician
The First Farmer / The Maidservant / The First King /
    The Second Princess / Another Farmer
The Second Farmer / The Priest / Hans-my-Hedgehog

The Juniper Tree

THE FIRST WIFE
THE SECOND WIFE
THE SON, *later* THE BEAUTIFUL BIRD
THE RICH MAN
THE DEVIL
MARLEENKEN
A GOLDSMITH
THE GOLDSMITH'S FIRST APPRENTICE
THE GOLDSMITH'S SECOND APPRENTICE
A SHOEMAKER
THE SHOEMAKER'S WIFE
THE MAID
THE MILLER'S FIRST APPRENTICE
THE MILLER'S SECOND APPRENTICE
THE MILLER'S THIRD APPRENTICE

This Tale can be told by a cast of four:
The First Wife / Marleenken (*puppet*) / The Goldsmith's Second
    Apprentice / The Maid / The Miller's First Apprentice
The Second Wife / The Shoemaker's Wife / The Goldsmith's
    First Apprentice / The Miller's Second Apprentice
The Son, *later* The Beautiful Bird (*puppet*)
The Rich Man / The Devil / A Goldsmith / A Shoemaker /
    The Miller's Third Apprentice

Little Red Riding Hood

For this Tale, it is important to distinguish between the two houses – one in which THE MOTHER *and* LITTLE RED RIDING HOOD *live; the other where* THE GRANDMOTHER *resides – and the perilous path that lies between them, through the woods. It would be useful to have some way of* THE GRANDMOTHER *– and later* LITTLE RED RIDING HOOD *– being able to disappear into the bed, ready to emerge later.*

THE MOTHER. Once upon a time

LITTLE RED RIDING HOOD. there was a little girl

THE HUNTSMAN. who was so sweet and kind

THE WOLF. that everyone loved her.

THE GRANDMOTHER. Her grandmother, who loved her more than anyone, gave her a little cap made of red velvet,

And she does.

LITTLE RED RIDING HOOD. which suited her so well that she wanted to wear it all the time.

So she slips this on.

THE WOLF. Because of that everyone took to calling her

LITTLE RED RIDING HOOD. Little Red Riding Hood.

THE HUNTSMAN. One day her mother said to her:

THE MOTHER. 'Little Red Riding Hood, I've got a job for you. Your grandmother isn't very well, and I want you to take her this cake and a bottle of wine. They'll make her feel a lot better. You be polite when you go into her house, and give her a kiss from me. Be careful on the way there, and don't step off the path or you might trip over and break the bottle and drop the cake, and then there'd be nothing for her. When you go into her parlour don't forget to say, "Good morning, Granny," and don't go peering in all the corners.'

LITTLE RED RIDING HOOD. 'I'll do everything right, don't worry,'

THE HUNTSMAN. said Little Red Riding Hood,

THE MOTHER. and kissed her mother goodbye.

Basket in hand, LITTLE RED RIDING HOOD *sets off on her journey.*

THE HUNTSMAN. Her grandmother lived in the woods, about half an hour's walk away.

THE WOLF. When Little Red Riding Hood had only been walking a few minutes, a wolf came up to her.

THE MOTHER. She didn't know what a wicked animal he was, so she wasn't afraid of him.

THE WOLF. 'Good morning, Little Red Riding Hood!'

THE HUNTSMAN. said the wolf.

LITTLE RED RIDING HOOD. 'Thank you, wolf, and good morning to you.'

THE WOLF. 'Where are you going so early this morning?'

LITTLE RED RIDING HOOD. 'To Granny's house.'

THE WOLF. 'And what's in that basket of yours?'

LITTLE RED RIDING HOOD. 'Granny's not very well, so I'm taking her some cake and some wine. We baked the cake yesterday, and it's full of good things like flour and eggs, and it'll be good for her and make her feel better.'

THE WOLF. 'Where does your granny live, Little Red Riding Hood?'

LITTLE RED RIDING HOOD. 'Well, I have to walk along this path till I come to three big oak trees, and there's her house, behind a hedge of hazel bushes. It's not very far away, about fifteen minutes' walk, I suppose. You must know the place.'

THE HUNTSMAN. The wolf thought,

THE WOLF (*circling his prey*). 'Now, this dainty young thing looks a very tasty mouthful. She'll taste even better than the old woman, but if I'm careful I'll be able to eat them both.'

THE MOTHER. So he walked along a while with Little Red Riding Hood, and then he said,

THE WOLF. 'Look at those flowers, Little Red Riding Hood! Aren't they lovely? The ones under the trees over there. Why don't you go closer so you can see them properly? And you seem as though you're walking to school, all serious and determined. You'll never hear the birds if you go along like that. It's so lovely in the woods – it's a shame not to enjoy it.'

THE HUNTSMAN. Little Red Riding Hood looked where he was pointing,

LITTLE RED RIDING HOOD. and when she saw the sunbeams dancing here and there between the trees, and how the beautiful flowers grew everywhere,

THE HUNTSMAN. she thought,

LITTLE RED RIDING HOOD. 'I could gather some flowers to take to Granny! She'll be very pleased with those. And it's still early – I've got time to do that and still be home on time.'

THE MOTHER (*with a parent's regret, at letting a child out alone*). So she stepped off the path,

LITTLE RED RIDING HOOD (*oblivious to the danger*). and ran into the trees to pick some flowers;

THE HUNTSMAN. but each time she picked one she saw an even prettier one a bit further away,

LITTLE RED RIDING HOOD. so she ran to get that as well.

THE HUNTSMAN. And all the time she went further and further into the wood.

THE WOLF. But while she was doing that, the wolf ran straight to the grandmother's house and knocked on the door.

Knock knock knock.

THE GRANDMOTHER. 'Who's there?'

THE WOLF. 'Little Red Riding Hood. I've got some cake and wine for you. Open the door!'

THE GRANDMOTHER. 'Just lift the latch. I'm feeling too weak to get out of bed.'

THE WOLF. The wolf lifted the latch and the door opened.

THE HUNTSMAN. He went inside, looked around to see where she was,

THE GRANDMOTHER (*horrified*). and then leaped on the grandmother's bed

THE WOLF. and ate her all up in one big gulp.

THE HUNTSMAN. Then he put on her clothes and put her nightcap on his head, and pulled the curtains tight shut,

THE WOLF. and got into bed.

LITTLE RED RIDING HOOD. All that time, Little Red Riding Hood had been wandering about picking flowers.

THE HUNTSMAN. Once she had gathered so many that she couldn't hold any more,

LITTLE RED RIDING HOOD. she remembered what she was supposed to be doing, and set off along the path to her grandmother's house.

THE HUNTSMAN. She had a surprise when she got there, because

LITTLE RED RIDING HOOD. the door was open and the room was dark. 'My goodness,'

THE HUNTSMAN. she thought,

LITTLE RED RIDING HOOD. 'I don't like this. I feel afraid and I usually like it at Granny's house.'

THE HUNTSMAN. She called out,

LITTLE RED RIDING HOOD. 'Good morning, Granny!'

THE HUNTSMAN. but there was no answer.

LITTLE RED RIDING HOOD. She went to the bed and pulled open the curtains.

THE HUNTSMAN. There was her grandmother, lying with her cap pulled down and looking very strange.

LITTLE RED RIDING HOOD. 'Oh, Granny, what big ears you've got!'

THE WOLF. 'All the better to hear you with.'

LITTLE RED RIDING HOOD. 'Granny, what big eyes
you've got!'

THE WOLF. 'All the better to see you with.'

LITTLE RED RIDING HOOD. 'And, Granny, what big hands
you've got!'

THE WOLF. 'All the better to hold you with.'

LITTLE RED RIDING HOOD. 'And oh, Granny, what a great
grim ghastly mouth you've got – '

THE WOLF. 'All the better to eat you with!'

THE HUNTSMAN. And as soon as the wolf said that, he
leaped out of bed and gobbled up Little Red Riding Hood.

THE WOLF. Once he'd swallowed her he felt full and satisfied,
and since the bed was so nice and soft, he climbed back in,
fell deeply asleep, and began to snore very loudly indeed.

At this point in the original production, THE
GRANDMOTHER (*played by the same actress as*
THE MOTHER) *and* LITTLE RED RIDING HOOD
emerged to witness the downfall of THE WOLF, *as well
as to make a live snoring sound with amplified bellows.
If you have a larger cast, you could keep them out of sight
here, and* LITTLE RED RIDING HOOD*'s next three lines
can be said by* THE MOTHER.

THE MOTHER. Just then a huntsman was passing by.

THE HUNTSMAN. 'The old woman's making such a noise,'

LITTLE RED RIDING HOOD. he thought,

THE HUNTSMAN. 'I'd better go and see if she's all right.'

THE MOTHER. He went into the parlour, and when he came
near the bed he stopped in astonishment.

THE HUNTSMAN. 'You old sinner! I've been looking for you
for a long time. Found you at last!'

LITTLE RED RIDING HOOD. He raised his rifle to his
shoulder,

THE MOTHER. but then he put it down again,

THE HUNTSMAN. because it occurred to him that the wolf might have eaten the old lady, and he might be able to rescue her.

LITTLE RED RIDING HOOD. So he put down the rifle

THE HUNTSMAN. and took a pair of scissors,

THE MOTHER. and began to snip open the wolf's bulging belly.

THE HUNTSMAN. After only a couple of snips he saw the red velvet cap, and a few snips later the girl jumped out.

And she does.

LITTLE RED RIDING HOOD. 'Oh, that was horrible! I was so frightened! It was so dark in the wolf's belly!'

THE HUNTSMAN. And then the grandmother began to clamber out,

THE GRANDMOTHER. a bit out of breath but not much the worse for her experience.

THE HUNTSMAN. While the hunter helped her to a chair,

LITTLE RED RIDING HOOD. Little Red Riding Hood ran outside to fetch some heavy stones.

THE HUNTSMAN. They filled the wolf's body with them,

LITTLE RED RIDING HOOD. and then Little Red Riding Hood sewed him up very neatly,

THE GRANDMOTHER. and then they woke him up.

THE WOLF. Seeing the hunter there with his gun, the wolf panicked and ran outside,

THE HUNTSMAN. but he didn't get very far.

LITTLE RED RIDING HOOD. The stones were so heavy that soon he fell down dead.

THE WOLF (*with his dying breath*). All three of them were very happy.

THE HUNTSMAN. The hunter skinned the wolf and went home with the pelt,

THE GRANDMOTHER. Granny ate the cake and drank the wine,

THE MOTHER. and Little Red Riding Hood thought,

LITTLE RED RIDING HOOD. 'What a narrow escape! As long as I live, I'll never do that again. (*Looking back towards the woods*.) If Mother tells me to stay on the path, that's exactly what I'll do.'

Rapunzel

This Tale starts with two key locations: the home of THE
HUSBAND *and his* WIFE, *and the high-walled garden of*
THE WITCH (*who, in the original production, was akin to an
eccentric allotment gardener*). *Later, there's a tower – in the
original production, this was achieved by a shift in perspective:
this fortress was laid out across the floor, with* RAPUNZEL*'s
hair symbolised by thick hemp rope. The children were puppets
– but don't have to be.*

THE PRINCE. There once lived a husband and wife

THE WIFE. who longed to have a child,

THE HUSBAND. but they longed in vain for quite some time.

THE WIFE. At last, however, the wife noticed unmistakable
signs

THE HUSBAND. that God had granted their wish.

THE WITCH. Now in the wall of their house there was a little
window that overlooked a magnificent garden full of every
kind of fruit and vegetable.

THE WIFE. There was a high wall around that garden,

THE HUSBAND. and no one dared go into it, because it
was the property of a very powerful witch who was feared
by everyone.

THE PRINCE. One day the woman was standing at that
window, and she saw

THE WIFE. a bed of lamb's lettuce,

THE WITCH. or rapunzel.

THE PRINCE. It looked

THE WIFE. so fresh and so green

THE PRINCE. that she longed to taste some,

THE WITCH. and this longing grew stronger every day,

THE HUSBAND. so that eventually she became really ill.

THE PRINCE. Her husband was alarmed at her condition, and said,

THE HUSBAND. 'My dear wife, what is the matter?'

THE WIFE. 'Oh, if I can't have any of that rapunzel in the garden behind our house, I'll die.'

THE PRINCE. The man loved his wife dearly, and he thought,

THE HUSBAND. 'Rather than let her die, I must get her some of that rapunzel. I don't care what it costs.'

THE PRINCE. So as night was falling he climbed over the high wall and got into the witch's garden, where he pulled up a handful of rapunzel.

THE HUSBAND. He scrambled back hastily and took it to his wife,

THE WIFE. who made it into a salad at once, and ate it hungrily. It tasted good.

THE WITCH. In fact it tasted so good that her desire for it grew stronger and stronger,

THE HUSBAND. and she begged her husband to

THE WIFE. go and get some more.

THE HUSBAND. So once again, just as it was getting dark, he set off and climbed the wall.

THE PRINCE. But when he set foot on the ground and turned to go to the bed of rapunzel, he had a shock,

THE HUSBAND (*frozen in fear*). for there was the witch standing in front of him.

THE WITCH (*glaring at him*). 'So you're the wretch who's been stealing my rapunzel! You'll pay for this, let me tell you.'

THE HUSBAND. 'That's fair, I can't argue with that, but let me plead for mercy. I had to do this. My wife saw your rapunzel from our window up there, and she felt a craving – you know how it is; it was so strong she thought she might die if she couldn't have some. So I had no choice.'

THE WITCH. The witch understood the reason.

THE PRINCE. The anger went out of her expression, and she nodded.

THE WITCH. 'I see. Well, if that's the case, you can have as much rapunzel as you want. But there's a condition: the child your wife is bearing shall belong to me. It will be perfectly safe; I shall look after it like a mother.'

THE HUSBAND. In his fear the man agreed to this, and hurried back home with the rapunzel.

THE WIFE *gasps, and clutches herself.*

THE PRINCE. And when in due course the wife gave birth,

THE HUSBAND. the witch appeared by her bed

THE WIFE. and took up the little girl in her arms.

THE WITCH. 'I name this child Rapunzel,'

THE HUSBAND. she said,

THE WIFE. and vanished with her.

At this point in the original production, THE WIFE *metamorphosised into the child:* RAPUNZEL.

THE PRINCE (*enchanted by her beauty*). Rapunzel grew up to become the most beautiful child the sun had ever shone on.

RAPUNZEL. When she was twelve years old, the witch took her into the depths of the forest

THE WITCH (*sealing the young girl in, with each phrase*). and shut her in a tower that had no door, no stairs and no windows

THE PRINCE. except one very small one in a room right at the top.

The ritual of climbing the tower.

THE HUSBAND. When the witch wanted to go in she would call:

THE WITCH.
'Rapunzel, Rapunzel,
Let down your hair.'

THE PRINCE. Rapunzel had beautiful hair,

THE HUSBAND. as fine as spun gold,

THE PRINCE. and of the same lustrous colour.

RAPUNZEL. When she heard the witch calling, she untied her hair and fastened it around the window hook before letting down its full length

THE HUSBAND. all the way to the ground,

THE PRINCE. twenty yards down,

THE WITCH. whereupon the witch climbed up it to her little room.

THE HUSBAND. After she had been in the tower for some years, it happened that the king's son was riding through the forest.

THE PRINCE. As he came near the tower he heard a song so lovely that he had to stop and listen to it.

And we listen, too, to this enchanting melody.

THE HUSBAND. Of course it was the lonely Rapunzel,

RAPUNZEL. singing to pass the time,

THE WITCH. and she had a sweet voice, too.

THE PRINCE. The prince wanted to go up to her, but there was no door to be found. He was baffled, and he rode home determined to come again and see if there was another way to get up the tower.

THE HUSBAND. Next day he came back, but with no more success.

THE PRINCE. Such a beautiful song, and no singer to be seen!

THE HUSBAND. But while he was pondering, he heard

THE PRINCE. someone coming

THE HUSBAND. and hid behind a tree.

RAPUNZEL. It was the witch.

THE PRINCE. When she was at the base of the tower, the prince heard her call out:

THE WITCH.
'Rapunzel, Rapunzel,
Let down your hair.'

THE PRINCE. To his astonishment, down from the window tumbled a length of golden hair.

THE WITCH. The witch seized hold and climbed all the way up, and clambered in through the window.

THE PRINCE. 'Well – if that's the way up, I'll try my luck with it.'

THE HUSBAND. So the following day, as darkness was falling, he went to the tower and called out:

THE PRINCE.
'Rapunzel, Rapunzel,
Let down your hair.'

THE WITCH. Down came the hair,

THE PRINCE. and the prince took its fragrant thickness into his hands and climbed up and jumped in through the window.

THE HUSBAND. At first Rapunzel was terrified.

RAPUNZEL. She had never seen a man before. He was nothing like the witch, so he was strange and unfamiliar to her, but he was so handsome that she was confused and didn't know what to say.

THE WITCH. However, a prince is never lost for words,

THE PRINCE. and he begged her not to be frightened. He explained how he'd heard her lovely voice singing from the tower, and how he couldn't rest until he found the singer; and how, now that he'd seen her, he found her face even more beautiful than her voice.

RAPUNZEL. Rapunzel was charmed by this, and soon lost her fear. Instead she felt delight in the young prince's company, and eagerly agreed to let him visit her again.

THE HUSBAND. Before many days had gone by their friendship had developed into love,

THE PRINCE (*on bended knee*). and when the prince asked her to marry him,

RAPUNZEL. Rapunzel consented at once.

THE HUSBAND. As for the witch, she suspected nothing at first.

THE WITCH. But one day Rapunzel said to her,

RAPUNZEL. 'You know, it's funny, but my clothes no longer fit me. Every dress I have is too tight.'

THE HUSBAND. The witch knew at once what that meant.

THE WITCH. 'You wicked girl! You've deceived me! All this time you've been entertaining a lover, and now we see the consequences! Well, I shall put an end to that.'

THE PRINCE. She took Rapunzel's beautiful hair in her left hand and snatched up some scissors with her right, and

THE WITCH. *snip-snap*!

RAPUNZEL. and down fell the lustrous strands up which the prince had climbed.

THE WITCH. The witch then transported Rapunzel by magic to a wild place far away.

THE PRINCE. There the poor young woman suffered greatly

RAPUNZEL. and, after a few months, gave birth to twins,

And the children emerge from behind her skirts.

RAPUNZEL'S SON. a boy

RAPUNZEL'S DAUGHTER. and a girl.

RAPUNZEL. They lived like tramps:

RAPUNZEL'S DAUGHTER. they had no money,

RAPUNZEL'S SON. no home,

RAPUNZEL. and only what they could beg from passers-by who heard Rapunzel sing.

She sings her lament as they crouch, hands outstretched.

RAPUNZEL'S SON. They were often hungry:

RAPUNZEL. in the winter they nearly perished of the cold,

RAPUNZEL'S DAUGHTER. and in the summer they were scorched by the burning sun.

THE PRINCE. But back to the tower.

THE HUSBAND. On the evening of the day when Rapunzel's hair was cut off, the prince came to the tower as usual and called:

THE PRINCE.
'Rapunzel, Rapunzel,
Let down your hair.'

RAPUNZEL. The witch was lying in wait. She had tied Rapunzel's hair to the window hook, and when she heard him call, she threw it down as the girl had done.

THE WITCH. The prince climbed up,

THE PRINCE. but instead of his beloved Rapunzel, at the window he found an ugly old woman, demented with anger, whose eyes flashed with fury as she railed at him:

THE WITCH. 'You're her fancy-boy, are you? You worm your way into the tower, you worm your way into her affections, you worm your way into her bed, you rogue, you leech, you lounge-lizard, you high-born mongrel! Well, the bird's not in her nest any more! The cat got her. What d'you think of that, eh? And the cat'll scratch your pretty eyes out too before she's finished. Rapunzel's gone, you understand? You'll never see her again!'

THE HUSBAND. And the witch forced the prince backwards and backwards until he fell out of the window.

THE PRINCE. A thorn bush broke his fall,

RAPUNZEL. but at the terrible cost of piercing his eyes.

He cries out, as he is blindfolded with a bloody bandage.

THE HUSBAND. Blinded in body and broken in spirit, the prince wandered away.

THE PRINCE. He lived as a beggar for some time, not knowing which country he was in.

Singing again.

RAPUNZEL. But one day

THE PRINCE. he heard a familiar voice,

RAPUNZEL. a voice that he loved,

THE PRINCE. and stumbled towards it.

RAPUNZEL'S DAUGHTER. And as he did so he heard

THE SON *and* THE DAUGHTER. two more voices joining in,

THE PRINCE. the voices of children –

RAPUNZEL'S SON. and suddenly they stopped singing,

RAPUNZEL. for their mother Rapunzel had recognised the prince

RAPUNZEL'S DAUGHTER. and was running towards him.

RAPUNZEL. They embraced,

RAPUNZEL'S SON. both of them crying with joy;

RAPUNZEL'S DAUGHTER. and then two of Rapunzel's tears fell into the prince's eyes,

RAPUNZEL'S SON. and his vision became clear once more.

And the blindfold is removed.

THE PRINCE. He saw his dear Rapunzel,

RAPUNZEL. and he saw his two children for the first time.

He scoops up his children in his arms.

RAPUNZEL'S DAUGHTER. So, reunited, they travelled back to the prince's kingdom,

RAPUNZEL'S SON. where they were welcomed;

THE PRINCE. and there they lived

RAPUNZEL. for the rest of their long and happy lives.

A final moment. THE WITCH – *who has been excluded from this last part of the story – alone, in her garden.*

The Three Snake Leaves

This story is a mini-epic, taking in numerous locations – so it is important to be able to move deftly between these. Ritual is key, throughout: in the marriage which becomes a funeral; in the sequence with dwindling supplies in the prison; in the slaying and resurrection of the snake, and of the others; and in the punishment meted out by THE KING. *The fairy tale rule of three is critical, too.*

THE PRINCESS. Once

THE POOR MAN. there was a poor man who couldn't support his only son any more.

THE PRINCESS. When the son realised this, he said,

THE SON. 'Father, it's no use my staying here. I'm just a burden to you. I'm going to leave home and see if I can earn a living.'

THE POOR MAN. The father gave him his blessing,

THE SON. and they parted sorrowfully.

THE KING. The king of a nearby country was a powerful ruler, and at that time he was waging war.

THE SON. The young man enlisted in his army – (*Salutes.*) and soon found himself at the front where a great battle was being fought.

Suddenly, we are in the midst of fierce combat.

THE SECOND SOLDIER. The bullets flew like hail,

THE THIRD SOLDIER. the danger was hideous,

THE SOLDIER (*as we must now call* THE SON). and his comrades were falling dead all around.

THE KING. When the general himself fell dead, the last of the troops were going to flee,

THE SECOND SOLDIER. but the young man took his place and yelled:

THE SOLDIER. 'We won't be defeated! Follow me, and God save the king!'

THE THIRD SOLDIER. The men followed him as he led the charge,

THE SECOND SOLDIER. and they soon had the enemy on the run.

Cheers of victory among the troops.

THE KING. When the king heard of the young man's part in the victory, he promoted him to field marshal,

THE SECOND SOLDIER. gave him gold and treasure,

THE POOR MAN (*proud of his son's success*). and bestowed on him the highest honours in the kingdom.

THE PRINCESS. Now the king had a daughter

THE SOLDIER (*as he sees her*). who was very beautiful,

THE KING. but she had one strange obsession.

THE POOR MAN. She had sworn an oath not to marry any man unless he promised to let himself be buried alive with her if she died first.

THE PRINCESS. 'After all, if he really loves me, why would he want to go on living?'

THE KING. And she said that she would do the same and be buried with him if he was the first to die.

THE POOR MAN. This grim condition had put off many young men who would otherwise have begged to marry her,

THE SOLDIER. but the soldier was so struck by her beauty that nothing would discourage him.

THE PRINCESS. So he asked the king for her hand.

THE KING. 'Do you know what you must promise?'

THE SOLDIER. 'If she dies before me, I must go to the grave with her. But I love her so much that I'm willing to risk that.'

THE KING. The king consented, and the wedding was celebrated with great splendour.

The lifting of the white veil; a kiss…

THE POOR MAN. For a while they lived together happily,

THE SOLDIER. but one day the princess fell ill.

… and she collapses in her husband's arms.

THE PRINCESS. Doctors came from all over the kingdom,

THE SOLDIER. but none of them could help her,

THE KING. and presently she died.

Her body is laid out, and the wedding veil becomes a funeral shroud.

THE SOLDIER. And then the young soldier remembered the promise he'd had to make, and shuddered.

THE POOR MAN. There was no way of getting out of it, even if he'd wanted to break the promise,

THE SOLDIER. because the king was going to put sentries at the grave itself and all around the cemetery in case he tried to escape.

THE KING. When the day came for the princess to be buried,

THE SOLDIER. they carried her body to the royal vault,

THE POOR MAN. made sure the young man was inside,

THE KING. and the king personally locked and bolted the door.

And the door to the royal vault slams shut.

THE SOLDIER. They had put some provisions in there: on a table there were four candles, four loaves of bread and four bottles of wine.

These are held up. There follows a ritual to highlight THE SOLDIER's *diminishing supplies: with each line of text, a shorter candle, a smaller piece of bread and a bottle containing less wine is held up – with each* STORYTELLER *relating to one item. In the original production, with a small cast,* THE PRINCESS *slipped out from under her funeral shroud here, to advance the story.*

THE PRINCESS. The soldier sat there beside the princess's body day after day,

THE POOR MAN. taking only a mouthful of bread and a sip of wine,

THE SOLDIER. making them last as long as possible.

THE PRINCESS. When he'd taken the last sip but one

THE POOR MAN. and eaten the last mouthful but one,

THE KING. and when the last candle was down to its last inch,

THE SOLDIER. he knew that his time had nearly come.

THE POOR MAN. But as he sat there in despair,

THE SOLDIER. he saw a snake crawl out of a corner of the vault and move towards the body.

And it does, manipulated by three STORYTELLERS.

THE KING. Thinking it intended to eat her, the young man drew his sword.

THE SOLDIER. 'While I live, you shan't touch her!'

THE PRINCESS. he said,

THE POOR MAN. and struck the snake three times,

THE KING. cutting it to pieces.

THE POOR MAN. Shortly afterwards, a second snake came crawling out of the corner.

This is handled by THE KING.

THE SOLDIER. It came to the body of the first snake, and looked at it, piece by piece,

THE PRINCESS. and then crawled away again.

THE SOLDIER. Soon it came back, and this time it had three green leaves in its mouth.

THE POOR MAN. Carefully moving the first snake's body together again,

THE KING. it laid a leaf on each of the wounds,

THE SOLDIER. and in a moment the dead snake stirred into life, the wounds closed up, and it was whole again.

THE PRINCESS. The two snakes hurried away together.

THE SOLDIER. But the leaves were still lying where they'd left them,

THE KING. and the young man thought

THE SOLDIER. that if their miraculous power had brought the snake back to life, it might do the same for a human being.

THE PRINCESS *slips back under the shroud.*

THE POOR MAN. So he picked up the leaves and laid them on the dead princess's white face,

THE KING. one on her mouth

THE POOR MAN. and the other two on her eyes.

THE SOLDIER. And as soon as he did this, her blood began to stir. A healthy pink came into her cheeks, and she drew a breath and opened her eyes.

THE PRINCESS (*gasping for air*). 'God in heaven! Where am I?'

THE SOLDIER. 'You're with me, my dear wife,'

THE KING. said the soldier,

THE POOR MAN. and told her all that had happened.

THE SOLDIER. He gave her the very last mouthful of bread and the very last sip of wine,

THE PRINCESS. and then they banged on the door

THE SOLDIER. and shouted so loudly

A SENTRY. that the sentries outside heard them and went running to the king.

THE KING. The king came to the graveyard himself and personally unlocked and unbolted the door of the vault.

A SENTRY. The princess tumbled into his arms,

THE SOLDIER. he shook the young man's hand,

THE PRINCESS. and everyone rejoiced at the miracle that had brought her back to life.

THE KING. As for the snake leaves, the soldier was a careful man,

THE SOLDIER. and he told no one about how the princess had been revived.

THE SERVANT. But he had an honest and reliable servant,

THE PRINCESS. so he gave this servant the three snake leaves to look after.

THE SOLDIER. 'Take good care of them – and make sure you keep them with you wherever we go. You never know when we might need them again.'

THE KING. Now after she was brought back to life, a change came over the princess.

THE SERVANT. All the love she had for her husband drained away from her heart.

THE PRINCESS. She still pretended to love him, however,

THE SOLDIER. and when he suggested making a sea voyage to visit his old father, she agreed at once.

THE PRINCESS. 'What a pleasure it'll be to meet the noble father of my dearest husband!'

And they embark on this journey.

THE SERVANT. But once at sea she forgot the great devotion the young man had shown her,

THE PRINCESS. because she felt a lust growing in her

THE CAPTAIN. for the captain of the ship.

THE SERVANT. Nothing would satisfy her but to sleep with him,

THE PRINCESS. and soon they were lovers.

THE CAPTAIN. One night in his arms she whispered,

THE PRINCESS. 'Oh, if only my husband were dead! What a marriage we two would make!'

THE CAPTAIN. 'That is easily arranged.'

THE PRINCESS. He took a length of cord

THE CAPTAIN. and, with the princess at his side, crept into the cabin where the young man was sleeping.

THE PRINCESS. The princess held one end of the cord

THE CAPTAIN. and the captain wound the other around her
husband's neck,

THE SOLDIER (*awaking, and finding that he is being choked*).
and then they pulled so hard that, struggle as he might, he
couldn't fight them off,

THE CAPTAIN. and soon they had strangled him.

THE PRINCESS. The princess took her dead husband by
the head

THE CAPTAIN. and the captain took him by the feet,

and they

THE PRINCESS *and* THE CAPTAIN.
threw him

THE PRINCESS.
over the ship's rail.

THE PRINCESS. 'Let's go home now. I'll tell my father that
he died at sea, and I'll sing your praises, and he'll let us be
married and you can inherit the kingdom.'

THE SERVANT (*emerging from the shadows*). But the faithful
servant had seen everything they'd done, and as soon as their
backs were turned he untied a boat from the ship and rowed
back in search of his master's body.

THE KING. He soon found it,

THE SERVANT. and after hauling it into the boat he untied the
cord from around the young man's neck

THE KING. and put the three snake leaves on his eyes
and mouth,

THE SOLDIER. and he came back to life at once.

THE SERVANT. Then the two of them rowed with all
their might.

THE SOLDIER. Day and night they rowed,

THE SERVANT. stopping for nothing,

THE SOLDIER. and their boat flew over the waves so fast

THE SERVANT. that they reached the shore a day before the ship,

THE SOLDIER. and went straight to the palace.

THE SERVANT. The king was amazed to see them.

THE KING. 'What's happened? Where's my daughter?'

THE SOLDIER. They told him everything,

THE SERVANT. and he was shocked to hear of his daughter's treachery.

THE KING. 'I can't believe she'd do such a terrible thing! But the truth will soon come to light.'

THE SOLDIER. And so it did.

THE KING. Very soon the ship arrived at the port,

THE SERVANT. and on hearing of this the king made the young man and his servant wait in a hidden room,

THE SOLDIER. where they could listen to everything that was said.

THE PRINCESS. The princess, dressed all in black, came sobbing to her father.

THE KING. 'Why have you come back alone? Where's your husband? And why are you wearing mourning?'

THE PRINCESS. 'Oh, Father dear, I'm inconsolable! My husband took ill with the yellow fever and died. The captain and I had to bury him at sea. If he hadn't helped me, I don't know what I would have done. But the captain's such a good man – he looked after my dear husband when the fever was at its height, no matter what the danger. He can tell you all about it.'

THE KING. 'Oh, your husband's dead, is he? Let's see if I can bring him back to life.'

THE SERVANT. And he opened the door

THE SOLDIER. and invited the other two to come out.

THE KING. When the princess saw the young man, she fell to the ground as if she'd been struck by lightning.

THE PRINCESS. She tried to say that her husband must have been hallucinating in his fever, that he must have fallen into a coma so deep they mistook it for death;

THE SERVANT. but the servant produced the cord,

THE SOLDIER. and in the face of that evidence she had to admit her guilt.

THE PRINCESS (*sobbing*). 'Yes, we did it... but please, Father – show some mercy!'

THE KING. 'Don't speak to me of mercy. Your husband was ready to die in the grave with you, and he gave you back your life, but you killed him in his sleep. You'll get the punishment you deserve.'

THE SOLDIER. And she and the captain were put on board a ship

THE PRINCESS. with holes drilled in the hull,

THE CAPTAIN. and sent out over the stormy sea.

THE SOLDIER. Soon they sank with the ship,

THE SERVANT. and were never seen again.

Hans-my-Hedgehog

*This Tale is another involving numerous locations: the farm,
the forest and the two kingdoms being the most important
ones. As elsewhere, moving deftly between these is essential.
As mentioned in the introduction, we used wooden scrubbing
brushes attached to a duffle coat to depict the adult* HANS
(*the baby was a single one of these brushes, wrapped in
swaddling clothes*).

HANS-MY-HEDGEHOG. Once

THE FARMER. there was a farmer

THE MAIDSERVANT. who had all the money and land
he wanted,

THE WIFE. but despite his wealth there was one thing missing
from his life.

THE FARMER. He and his wife had never had any children.

THE WIFE. When he met other farmers in town or at the
market, they would often make fun of him and ask

THE FIRST FARMER. why he and his wife had never managed
to do what their cattle did regularly.

THE SECOND FARMER. Didn't they know how to do it?

THE MAIDSERVANT. In the end he lost his temper,

THE WIFE. and when he got back home, he swore and said,

THE FARMER. 'I will have a child, even if it's a hedgehog.'

HANS-MY-HEDGEHOG (*looking back on the scene of his
birth*). Not long afterwards his wife did have a child,

THE WIFE. a boy,

THE FARMER. as they could see from his bottom half.

THE MAIDSERVANT. The top half, though, was

THE FARMER. a hedgehog.

HANS-MY-HEDGEHOG. When she saw him, she was horrified.

THE WIFE. 'See what you've done! This is all your fault.'

THE FARMER. 'It can't be helped. We're stuck with him. He'll have to be baptised like a normal boy, but I don't know who we can ask to be godfather.'

THE WIFE. 'And the only name we can give him is... Hans-my-Hedgehog.'

THE MAIDSERVANT. When he was baptised, the priest said,

THE PRIEST. 'I don't know what you'll do for a bed. He can't sleep on a normal mattress, he'd jab holes all over it.'

THE FARMER. The farmer and his wife saw the truth of that,

THE WIFE. and put some straw down behind the stove and laid him there.

THE FARMER. His mother couldn't suckle him;

THE WIFE. she tried, but it was too painful altogether.

THE MAIDSERVANT. The little creature lay behind the stove for eight years, and his father grew sick to death of him.

THE FARMER. 'I wish he'd kick the bucket,'

THE MAIDSERVANT. he thought,

HANS-MY-HEDGEHOG. but Hans-my-Hedgehog didn't die;

THE WIFE. he just lay there.

THE MAIDSERVANT. One day there happened to be a fair in the town, and the farmer wanted to go.

THE FARMER. He asked his wife what she'd like him to bring back for her.

THE WIFE. 'A bit of steak and a half a dozen rolls.'

THE FARMER. Then he asked the maidservant, and she asked for

THE MAIDSERVANT. a pair of slippers and some fancy stockings.

THE WIFE. Finally he said to his son,

THE FARMER. 'Well, what would you like?'

HANS-MY-HEDGEHOG. 'Papa, I'd like some bagpipes.'

THE WIFE. When the farmer came back,

THE FARMER. he gave his wife the steak and the rolls,

THE MAIDSERVANT. he gave the maid the slippers
and stockings,

THE FARMER. and finally he went behind the stove and gave
Hans-my-Hedgehog his bagpipes.

THE MAIDSERVANT. Then Hans-my-Hedgehog said,

HANS-MY-HEDGEHOG. 'Papa, go to the blacksmith's and
have him make some shoes for the cockerel. Once you've
done that, I'll ride away and never come back.'

THE FARMER. The farmer was happy to get rid of him, so he
took the cockerel to the blacksmith's and had him shod.

HANS-MY-HEDGEHOG. Once that was done, Hans-my-
Hedgehog jumped on the cockerel's back and rode away,
taking some pigs with him to tend in the forest.

THE WIFE *follows her son a little way, to be sure that he
is safe.*

THE WIFE. When they were in the forest he spurred the
cockerel up, and it flew high into a tree with him.

HANS-MY-HEDGEHOG. There he sat keeping an eye on his
pigs and learning how to play the bagpipes.

THE WIFE. Years went by,

THE FARMER. and his father had no idea where he was;

HANS-MY-HEDGEHOG. but the herd grew bigger and bigger
and he played more and more skilfully.

THE WIFE. In fact the music he made was quite beautiful.

THE FIRST KING. One day a king came riding past.

HANS-MY-HEDGEHOG. He had lost his way in the forest,

THE FIRST KING. and he was amazed to hear such lovely music, so he stopped to listen to it.

THE SERVANT. He had no idea where it was coming from,

THE FIRST KING. so he sent a servant to find the musician.

A COURTIER. The servant looked around and finally came back to the king.

THE SERVANT. 'There's a strange little animal sitting up in that tree, your majesty. It looks like a cockerel with a hedgehog sitting on it. And the hedgehog's playing the bagpipes.'

THE FIRST KING. 'Well, go and ask it the way!'

THE SERVANT. The servant went and called up into the tree,

HANS-MY-HEDGEHOG. and Hans-my-Hedgehog stopped playing and climbed down to the ground.

THE SERVANT. He bowed to the king and said,

HANS-MY-HEDGEHOG. 'What can I do for you, your majesty?'

THE FIRST KING. 'You can tell me the way to my kingdom. I'm lost.'

HANS-MY-HEDGEHOG. 'With pleasure, your majesty. I'll tell you the way if you promise in writing to give me the first thing that greets you when you arrive home.'

A COURTIER. The king looked at him, and thought,

THE FIRST KING. 'That's easy enough to promise. This monster won't be able to read, so I can write anything.'

THE SERVANT. So he took pen and ink and wrote a few words on a piece of paper.

HANS-MY-HEDGEHOG. Hans-my-Hedgehog took it and showed him the way,

THE FIRST KING. and the king set off and was soon home again.

THE FIRST PRINCESS. Now the king had a daughter, and when she saw him coming back, she was overjoyed and ran down to greet him and kiss him.

THE FIRST KING. She was the first person he met on the way in, and of course the king thought about Hans-my-Hedgehog, and told his daughter how he had nearly had to promise her

HANS-MY-HEDGEHOG. to a strange animal

THE SERVANT. that sat on a cockerel

THE FIRST PRINCESS. and played the bagpipes.

THE FIRST KING. 'But don't you worry, my dear. I wrote something quite different. That hedgehog creature won't be able to read.'

THE FIRST PRINCESS. 'That's a good thing, because I wouldn't have gone with him anyway.'

HANS-MY-HEDGEHOG. Meanwhile, Hans-my-Hedgehog stayed in the forest enjoying himself, tending his pigs and playing his bagpipes.

THE FIRST KING. The forest happened to be very large,

THE SECOND KING. and not long afterwards another king came by, with all his servants and messengers,

THE MESSENGER. and he too was lost.

THE FIRST KING. Like the first king,

THE SECOND KING. he heard the beautiful music and sent a messenger to find out where it was coming from.

THE MESSENGER. The messenger saw Hans-my-Hedgehog up in the tree playing the bagpipes, and called up to ask what he was doing.

HANS-MY-HEDGEHOG. 'I'm keeping an eye on my pigs. What do you want?'

THE MESSENGER. The messenger explained,

HANS-MY-HEDGEHOG. and Hans-my-Hedgehog came down and told the old king that he'd tell him the way in exchange for a promise,

THE FIRST KING. and it was the same promise as before: the king must give him the first creature that greeted him when he got home.

THE SECOND KING. The king agreed, and signed a paper saying so.

HANS-MY-HEDGEHOG. Once that was done, Hans-my-Hedgehog rode ahead on the cockerel to show them the way to the edge of the forest, where he said goodbye to the king and went back to his pigs;

THE SECOND KING. and so the king came home safely,

THE MESSENGER. to the joy of all his courtiers.

THE SECOND PRINCESS. This king too had an only daughter,

HANS-MY-HEDGEHOG. who was very beautiful,

THE SECOND KING. and she was the first to run out

THE SECOND PRINCESS. and welcome her beloved father.

THE SECOND KING. She threw her arms around him and kissed him, and asked him

THE SECOND PRINCESS. where he'd been and why he'd taken so long.

THE SECOND KING. 'We lost our way, my love. But in the depths of the forest we came upon the strangest thing: a half-hedgehog, half-boy sitting on a cockerel and playing the bagpipes. Playing them remarkably well, too. He showed us the way, you see, and… Well, my dear, I had to promise to give him whoever came out to greet me first. Oh, my darling, I'm so terribly sorry.'

THE MESSENGER. But the princess loved her father,

THE SECOND PRINCESS. and said that she wouldn't make him break his promise; she would go with Hans-my-Hedgehog whenever he came for her.

HANS-MY-HEDGEHOG. Meanwhile, back in the forest, Hans-my-Hedgehog looked after his pigs.

An ever-growing litter is revealed, piglet by piglet.

A FARMER. And those pigs had more pigs,

ANOTHER FARMER. and then those pigs had more pigs,

A THIRD FARMER. until there were so many that the forest
was full of pigs from one end to the other.

HANS-MY-HEDGEHOG. At that point Hans-my-Hedgehog
decided that he'd spent all the time he wanted to in the forest.

THE MAIDSERVANT. He sent a message to his father, saying
that they should empty all the pigsties in the village,

THE WIFE. because he was coming with such a large herd of
pigs that anyone who wanted some pork or bacon could join
in and help themselves.

THE FARMER. His father was a bit put out to hear this.
He thought Hans-my-Hedgehog was dead and gone.

HANS-MY-HEDGEHOG. But then along came his son driving
all those pigs in front of him,

THE MAIDSERVANT. and the village had such a slaughter that
they could hear the noise two miles away.

THE WIFE. When it was all over Hans-my-Hedgehog said,

HANS-MY-HEDGEHOG. 'Papa, my cockerel needs new
shoes. If you take him to the blacksmith and have him shod
again, I'll ride away and never come back as long as I live.'

THE FARMER. So the farmer did that, and was relieved to
think that he'd seen the back of Hans-my-Hedgehog at last.

HANS-MY-HEDGEHOG. When the cockerel was ready,
Hans-my-Hedgehog jumped on his back and rode away.

THE SERVANT. He rode and rode till he came to the kingdom
of the first king,

THE FIRST KING. the king of the broken promise.

THE SERVANT (*proclaiming a royal decree*). The king had
given strict orders that if anyone approached the palace
playing the bagpipes and riding on a cockerel, they should be
shot, stabbed, bombed, knocked down, blown up, strangled,
anything to prevent them from entering.

THE FIRST KING. So when Hans-my-Hedgehog appeared, the
brigade of guards was ordered out to charge at him with
their bayonets.

HANS-MY-HEDGEHOG. But he was too quick for them. He spurred the cockerel up into the air and flew right over the top of the soldiers, over the palace wall and up to the king's window.

THE SERVANT. He perched there on the sill and shouted out that

HANS-MY-HEDGEHOG. he'd come for what he'd been promised, and that if the king tried to weasel out of it he'd pay for it with his life,

THE FIRST PRINCESS. and so would the princess.

THE FIRST KING. The king told his daughter that she'd better do what Hans-my-Hedgehog wanted.

THE FIRST PRINCESS. She put on a white dress,

THE FIRST KING. and the king hastily ordered a carriage with six fine horses to be made ready, and piled gold and silver and the deeds to several fine farms and forests into it, and ordered two dozen of his best servants to go with it.

THE SERVANT. The horses were harnessed, the servants were all lined up,

THE FIRST PRINCESS. the princess climbed in,

HANS-MY-HEDGEHOG. and then Hans-my-Hedgehog took his place beside her with the cockerel on his knee and the bagpipes on his lap.

THE SERVANT. They said

THE FIRST PRINCESS. goodbye

THE SERVANT. and off they went.

THE FIRST KING. The king thought he'd never see his daughter again.

HANS-MY-HEDGEHOG. He was wrong about that, though. As soon as they were out of the city, Hans-my-Hedgehog ordered the princess out of the carriage, and told the servants to take several paces backwards

THE SERVANT. and look the other way.

THE FIRST PRINCESS. Then he tore the princess's white dress into shreds and stuck her all over with his prickles until she was covered in blood.

HANS-MY-HEDGEHOG. 'That's what you get for trying to deceive me. Now clear off. Go home. You're no good to me, and I don't want you.'

THE FIRST PRINCESS. And she went home with the servants and the gold and the carriage and all, disgraced.

THE SECOND PRINCESS. So much for her.

HANS-MY-HEDGEHOG. As for Hans-my-Hedgehog, he took his bagpipes and jumped on the cockerel and rode away to the second kingdom, whose king had behaved very differently from the first one.

THE SECOND KING. He had given orders that if anyone arrived in the kingdom looking like a hedgehog and riding a cockerel, he should be saluted, given a cavalry escort, greeted with crowds cheering and waving flags, and brought with honour to the royal palace.

THE SECOND PRINCESS. The king had told his daughter what Hans-my-Hedgehog looked like, of course,

HANS-MY-HEDGEHOG. but when she saw him she was shocked all the same.

THE SECOND KING. However, there was nothing to be done about it; her father had given his word, and she had given hers.

THE SECOND PRINCESS. She bade Hans-my-Hedgehog welcome, with all her heart,

HANS-MY-HEDGEHOG. and they were married at once,

THE MESSENGER. and sat next to each other at the banquet.

HANS-MY-HEDGEHOG *and* THE SECOND PRINCESS *enjoy a wedding dance together. Tenderly. Carefully.*

THE SECOND PRINCESS. And then it was time to go to bed.

THE SECOND KING. He could see she was afraid of his prickles.

HANS-MY-HEDGEHOG. 'You mustn't be frightened. I'd do anything rather than hurt you.'

THE SECOND KING. He told the old king to have a large fire made in the fireplace on the landing, and to have four men ready outside the bedroom door.

HANS-MY-HEDGEHOG. 'I'm going to take off my hedgehog skin as soon as I go into the bedroom. The men must seize it at once and throw it on the fire, and stay there till it's all burnt to ash.'

THE SECOND PRINCESS. When the clock struck eleven, Hans-my-Hedgehog went into the bedroom, took off his skin, and laid it down by the bed.

THE SECOND KING. Immediately the four men rushed in, seized the prickly skin, flung it on the fire and stood around watching till it had all burned up,

HANS-MY-HEDGEHOG. and the moment the last prickle was consumed by the last flame, Hans was free. He lay down on the bed like a human being at last.

THE SECOND PRINCESS. However, he was scorched and charred all over, as if he himself had been in the fire.

THE SECOND KING. The king sent at once for the royal physician,

THE PHYSICIAN. who cleaned him up and tended to his skin with special balms and ointments, and soon he looked like an ordinary young man, though more handsome than most.

THE SECOND PRINCESS. The princess was overjoyed.

HANS-MY-HEDGEHOG. Next morning they both rose from the royal bed full of happiness,

THE SECOND PRINCESS. and when they had eaten breakfast they celebrated their wedding again;

HANS-MY-HEDGEHOG. and in time Hans-my-Hedgehog succeeded the old king, and inherited the kingdom.

THE SECOND PRINCESS. Some years later he took his wife all the way back to see his father.

THE FARMER. Of course the old farmer had no idea who
he was.

HANS-MY-HEDGEHOG. 'I'm your son,'

THE SECOND PRINCESS. said Hans-my-Hedgehog.

THE FARMER. 'Oh, no, no, that can't be right. I did have a
son, but he was like a hedgehog, all covered in prickles,

THE WIFE. and he went off to see the world a long time ago.'

THE SECOND PRINCESS. But Hans said that he was the one,

THE FARMER. and told so many details about his life

THE WIFE. that the farmer was finally convinced;

THE SECOND PRINCESS. and the old man wept for joy,

HANS-MY-HEDGEHOG. and returned with his son to
his kingdom.

The Juniper Tree

The tree is, of course, critical in this Tale. And also how to depict the children and the bird. In the original, both THE SON *and* MARLEENKEN *were puppets: they don't have to be, although the boy's decapitation is tricky without this approach.* THE BEAUTIFUL BIRD, *meanwhile, was a repurposed umbrella, crowned with a doll's head – and was operated by the storyteller who played* THE SON.

THE SON. Two thousand years ago,

THE SECOND WIFE. or a very long time anyway,

THE RICH MAN. there lived a rich man

THE FIRST WIFE. and his good and beautiful wife.

THE SON. They loved each other dearly.

THE SECOND WIFE. There was only one thing needed to complete their happiness,

THE FIRST WIFE. and that was children,

THE RICH MAN. but as much as they longed for a child,

THE FIRST WIFE. and as much as the woman prayed both day and night,

THE FIRST WIFE, THE SECOND WIFE *and* THE SON. no child came,

THE RICH MAN. and no child came.

THE SECOND WIFE. Now in front of their house was a courtyard, where there grew a juniper tree.

THE FIRST WIFE. One winter's day the woman stood under the tree peeling an apple,

THE SON. and as she did so she cut her finger, and a drop of blood fell into the snow.

THE FIRST WIFE (*sighing*). 'Oh, if only I had a child as red as blood and as white as snow!'

THE RICH MAN. As she said that

THE FIRST WIFE. her heart lifted, and she felt happy.

THE SON. She went back into the house, feeling sure everything would end well.

The STORYTELLERS *encircle the tree to witness the cycle of the seasons.*

THE RICH MAN. One month went by, and the snow vanished.

THE SECOND WIFE. Two months went by, and the world turned green.

THE FIRST WIFE. Three months went by, and flowers bloomed out of the earth.

THE SON. Four months went by, and all the twigs on all the trees in the forest grew stronger and pressed themselves together, and the birds sang so loud that the woods resounded, and the blossom fell from the trees.

THE RICH MAN. Five months went by,

THE SECOND WIFE. and the woman stood under the juniper tree.

THE FIRST WIFE. It smelled so sweet that her heart leaped in her breast, and she fell to her knees with joy.

THE SON. Six months went by,

THE RICH MAN. and the fruit grew firm and heavy, and the woman fell still.

THE SECOND WIFE. When seven months had gone by, she plucked the juniper berries

THE FIRST WIFE. and ate so many that she felt sick and sorrowful.

THE SON. After the eighth month had gone,

THE RICH MAN. she called her husband

THE SECOND WIFE. and said to him, weeping,

THE FIRST WIFE. 'If I die, bury me under the juniper tree.'

THE SON. She felt comforted by his promise,

THE RICH MAN. and then one more month went by,

THE SON. and she had a child

THE FIRST WIFE. as red as blood and as white as snow;

THE SECOND WIFE. when she saw the baby her heart could not contain her joy,

THE RICH MAN. and she died.

THE SON. Her husband buried her under the juniper tree, weeping bitterly.

The ghost of THE FIRST WIFE *lingers, in limbo, watching over her family.*

THE FIRST WIFE. After a little time his first anguish ebbed away,

THE RICH MAN. and although he still wept, it was less bitterly than before.

THE SECOND WIFE. And after a little more time had gone by, he took a second wife.

MARLEENKEN. He had a daughter by the second wife,

THE SON. but his first wife's child, as red as blood and as white as snow, was a son.

THE SECOND WIFE. The second wife loved her daughter, but whenever she looked at the little boy she felt her heart twist with hatred, because she knew he would inherit her husband's wealth, and she feared her daughter would get nothing.

THE DEVIL. Seeing this, the Devil got into her and let her think of nothing else,

MARLEENKEN. and from then on she never left the little boy alone:

THE SON. she slapped him and cuffed him,

MARLEENKEN. she shouted at him and made him

THE SECOND WIFE. stand in the corner,

THE SON. until the poor child was so afraid he hardly dared come home from school,

THE DEVIL. for there was nowhere he could find any peace.

THE SECOND WIFE. One day the woman had gone into the pantry when her little daughter Marleenken came in after her and said,

MARLEENKEN. 'Mama, can I have an apple?'

THE SECOND WIFE. 'Of course, my dear,'

THE DEVIL. said the woman, and gave her a fine red apple from the chest. (*Whispering an evil idea into* THE SECOND WIFE*'s ear.*) This chest had a heavy lid with a sharp iron lock.

MARLEENKEN. 'Mama, can my brother have one too?'

THE SECOND WIFE. Mention of the little boy made the woman angry,

THE DEVIL. but she contained herself and said,

THE SECOND WIFE. 'Yes, of course, when he comes home from school.'

MARLEENKEN. Just then she happened to look out of the window and saw the little boy coming home.

THE DEVIL. And it was as if the Devil himself entered her head, because she seized the apple from the girl and said,

THE SECOND WIFE. 'You're not going to have one before your brother.'

THE DEVIL. She threw the apple into the chest and shut it,

MARLEENKEN. and Marleenken went up to her room.

THE SON. Then the little boy came in,

THE DEVIL. and the Devil made the woman say sweetly,

THE SECOND WIFE. 'My son, would you like an apple?'

THE FIRST WIFE. But her eyes were fierce.

THE SON. 'Mama, you look so angry! Yes, I'd like an apple.'

THE DEVIL. She couldn't stop. She had to go on.

THE SECOND WIFE. 'Come with me,'

THE DEVIL. she said, opening the lid of the chest.

THE SECOND WIFE. 'Choose an apple for yourself. Lean right in – that's it – the best ones are at the back…'

THE DEVIL. And while the little boy was leaning in, the Evil One nudged her, and

THE SECOND WIFE. *bam*! She slammed down the lid, and his head fell off and rolled in among the red apples.

THE FIRST WIFE. Then she felt horribly afraid, and she thought,

THE SECOND WIFE. 'What can I do? But maybe there's a way…'

THE FIRST WIFE. And she ran upstairs to her chest of drawers

THE DEVIL. and took a white scarf, and then she sat the little boy in a chair by the kitchen door and set his head on his neck again, and tied the scarf around it so nothing could be seen.

THE SECOND WIFE. Then she put an apple in his hand, and went into the kitchen to put some water on the stove to boil.

THE FIRST WIFE. And Marleenken came into the kitchen and said,

MARLEENKEN. 'Mama, brother is sitting by the door, and he's got an apple in his hand, and his face is so white! I asked him to give me the apple, but he didn't answer me, and I was frightened.'

THE SECOND WIFE. 'Well, you go back out there and speak to him again: and if he won't answer you this time, smack his face.'

THE FIRST WIFE. So Marleenken went to the little boy and said,

MARLEENKEN. 'Brother, give me the apple.'

THE SON. But he sat still and said nothing,

MARLEENKEN. so she smacked his face,

THE DEVIL. and his head fell off.

THE FIRST WIFE. Poor Marleenken was terrified. She screamed and ran to her mother and cried,

MARLEENKEN. 'Oh, Mother, Mother, I've knocked my brother's head off!'

THE FIRST WIFE. She sobbed and cried and nothing would comfort her.

THE SECOND WIFE. 'Oh, Marleenken, you bad girl – what have you done? But be quiet, hush, don't say a word about it. It can't be helped. We won't tell anyone. We'll put him in the stew.'

THE FIRST WIFE. So she took the little boy

THE SECOND WIFE. and chopped him into pieces and put them in the pot.

MARLEENKEN. Marleenken couldn't stop crying;

THE SECOND WIFE. in fact so many tears fell in the water that there was no need for salt.

THE RICH MAN. Presently the father came home and sat down at the table.

And now THE SON *joins his mother as a ghostly presence in the kitchen.*

THE SON. He looked around and said,

THE RICH MAN. 'Where's my little boy?'

THE SECOND WIFE. The woman put a large dish of stew on the table.

MARLEENKEN. Marleenken was crying and crying helplessly.

THE SON. The father said again,

THE RICH MAN. 'Where's my son? Why isn't he here at the table?'

THE SECOND WIFE. 'Oh, he's gone away to visit his mother's great-uncle's family. He's going to stay with them for a while.'

THE RICH MAN. 'But why? He didn't even say goodbye.'

THE SECOND WIFE. 'He wanted to go. He said he was going to stay for six weeks. Don't worry, they'll look after him.'

THE RICH MAN. 'Well, I'm upset about that. He shouldn't have gone like that without asking me. I'm sorry he's not here. He should have said goodbye.'

THE SON. And he began to eat, and he said,

THE RICH MAN. 'Marleenken dear, why are you crying? Your brother will come back, don't worry.'

MARLEENKEN. And he ate some more stew, and then he said,

THE RICH MAN. 'Wife, this is the best stew I've ever tasted. It's delicious! Give me some more. You two aren't having any. I've got a feeling that this is all for me.'

THE SECOND WIFE. And he ate the whole dish, every scrap, and threw the bones under the table.

THE SON. Marleenken went to her chest of drawers

THE FIRST WIFE. and took out her best silk scarf.

THE SON. Then she gathered up all the bones from under the table, tied them up in the scarf,

MARLEENKEN. and took them outside.

THE SON. Her poor eyes had wept so much they had no tears left, and she could only cry blood.

THE FIRST WIFE. She laid the bones down on the green grass under the juniper tree,

MARLEENKEN. and as she did so she felt her heart lighten, and she stopped crying.

THE RICH MAN. And the juniper tree began to move.

THE SECOND WIFE. First the branches moved apart, and then they moved together again,

MARLEENKEN. like someone clapping their hands.

THE RICH MAN. As that happened a golden mist gathered among the branches and then rose up like a flame,

THE BIRD. and at the heart of the flame there was a beautiful bird that flew high into the air singing and chirping merrily.

THE SECOND WIFE. And when the bird was gone, the juniper tree was just as it had been before,

THE FIRST WIFE. but the scarf and the bones had vanished. Marleenken felt happy again,

MARLEENKEN. just as happy as if her brother was still alive, and she ran into the house and sat down to eat her supper.

THE BIRD. Meanwhile the bird was flying far away.

THE GOLDSMITH. He flew to a town and settled on the roof of a goldsmith's house and began to sing:

THE BIRD.
'My mother cut my head off,
My father swallowed me,
My sister buried all my bones
Under the juniper tree.
Keewitt! Keewitt! You'll never find
A prettier bird than me!'

THE GOLDSMITH. Inside his workshop the goldsmith was making a golden chain.

THE GOLDSMITH'S FIRST APPRENTICE. He heard the bird singing overhead and thought

THE GOLDSMITH. how lovely it sounded, so he stood up to run outside and see what sort of bird it could be.

THE GOLDSMITH'S SECOND APPRENTICE. He left the house in such a hurry one of his slippers fell off on the way, and he stood in the middle of the street in his leather apron

THE GOLDSMITH'S FIRST APPRENTICE. and one slipper,

THE GOLDSMITH'S SECOND APPRENTICE. with his pincers in one hand and the golden chain in the other,

THE GOLDSMITH'S FIRST APPRENTICE. and he looked up to see the bird and shaded his eyes from the bright sun and called out:

THE GOLDSMITH. 'Hey, bird! That's a lovely song you're singing! Sing it again for me!'

THE BIRD. 'Oh, no – I don't sing twice for nothing. Give me that golden chain and I'll sing it again for you.'

THE GOLDSMITH. 'Here you are, and welcome. Come and take it, but do sing that song again!'

THE GOLDSMITH'S SECOND APPRENTICE. The bird flew down and took the golden chain in his right claw, and perched on the garden fence and sang:

THE BIRD.
'My mother cut my head off,
My father swallowed me,
My sister buried all my bones
Under the juniper tree.
Keewitt! Keewitt! You'll never find
A prettier bird than me!'

THE SHOEMAKER'S WIFE. Then the bird flew away and found a shoemaker's house, and he perched on the roof and sang:

THE BIRD.
'My mother cut my head off,
My father swallowed me,
My sister buried all my bones
Under the juniper tree.
Keewitt! Keewitt! You'll never find
A prettier bird than me!'

THE SHOEMAKER. The shoemaker was tapping away at his last, but his hammer fell still as he heard the song, and he ran out of doors and looked up at the roof.

THE SHOEMAKER'S WIFE. He had to shade his eyes because the sun was so bright.

THE SHOEMAKER. 'Bird, you're a wonderful singer! I've never heard a song like it!'

THE SHOEMAKER'S WIFE. He ran back inside and called,

THE SHOEMAKER. 'Wife, come out and listen to this bird! He's a marvel!'

THE SHOEMAKER'S WIFE. He called his daughter and her children,

THE SHOEMAKER. and his apprentices,

THE MAID. and the maid,

THE SHOEMAKER. and they all came out into the street and gazed up in amazement.

THE SHOEMAKER'S WIFE. The bird's red and green feathers were shining,

THE SHOEMAKER. and the golden feathers of his neck were dazzling in the sunlight,

THE MAID. and his eyes sparkled like stars.

THE SHOEMAKER. 'Bird,'

THE SHOEMAKER'S WIFE. the shoemaker called up,

THE SHOEMAKER. 'sing that song again!'

THE BIRD. 'Oh, no – I don't sing twice for nothing. Give me those red slippers I can see on your bench.'

THE SHOEMAKER. The wife ran into the shop

THE MAID. and brought out the slippers,

THE BIRD. and the bird flew down and seized them in his left claw.

THE SHOEMAKER. Then he flew around their heads, singing:

THE BIRD.
'My mother cut my head off,
My father swallowed me,
My sister buried all my bones
Under the juniper tree.
Keewitt! Keewitt! You'll never find
A prettier bird than me!'

THE SHOEMAKER'S WIFE. Then he flew away, out of the town and along the river,

THE MAID. and in his right claw he had the golden chain

THE SHOEMAKER. and in his left he had the slippers.

THE BIRD. He flew and he flew till he came to a mill,

THE MILLER'S FIRST APPRENTICE. and the mill wheel was going

THE THREE APPRENTICES. clippety-clap, clippety-clap, clippety-clap.

THE MILLER'S SECOND APPRENTICE. Outside the mill twenty apprentices were sitting down chiselling a new millstone,

THE THREE APPRENTICES. hick-hack, hick-hack, hick-hack,

THE MILLER'S THIRD APPRENTICE. and the mill went

THE THREE APPRENTICES. clippety-clap, clippety-clap, clippety-clap.

THE MILLER'S THIRD APPRENTICE. The bird flew round and perched on a linden tree that stood in front of the mill, and began to sing:

THE BIRD.
   'My mother cut my head off – '

THE MILLER'S FIRST APPRENTICE. And one of the apprentices stopped working and looked up.

THE BIRD.
   'My father swallowed me – '

THE MILLER'S THIRD APPRENTICE. Two more stopped working and listened.

THE BIRD.
   'My sister buried all my bones – '

THE MILLER'S FIRST *and* SECOND APPRENTICES. Four of them stopped.

THE BIRD.
   'Under the juniper tree – '

THE MILLER'S FIRST *and* THIRD APPRENTICES. And eight put their chisels down.

THE BIRD.
   'Keewitt! Keewitt! You'll never find – '

THE THREE APPRENTICES. And now four more looked all around.

THE BIRD.
  'A prettier bird than me!'

THE MILLER'S THIRD APPRENTICE. Finally the last
  apprentice heard, and dropped his chisel, and then all twenty

THE THREE APPRENTICES. burst into cheers

THE MILLER'S FIRST APPRENTICE. and clapped

THE MILLER'S SECOND APPRENTICE. and threw their hats
  in the air.

THE MILLER'S THIRD APPRENTICE. 'Bird,'

THE MILLER'S FIRST APPRENTICE. cried the last
  apprentice,

THE MILLER'S THIRD APPRENTICE. 'that's the best song
  I've ever heard! But I only heard the last line. Sing it again
  for me!'

THE BIRD. 'Oh, no – I don't sing twice for nothing. Give me
  that millstone you're all working on, and I'll sing you the
  song again.'

THE MILLER'S SECOND APPRENTICE. 'If it only belonged
  to me, you could have it like a shot! But...'

THE MILLER'S FIRST APPRENTICE. 'Oh, come on,'

THE MILLER'S THIRD APPRENTICE. said the others.

THE MILLER'S FIRST APPRENTICE. 'If he sings again, he
  can have it and welcome.'

THE MILLER'S SECOND APPRENTICE. So the twenty
  apprentices took a long beam

THE MILLER'S THIRD APPRENTICE. and laid the end under
  the edge of the millstone

THE MILLER'S FIRST APPRENTICE. and heaved it up:

THE THREE APPRENTICES. Heave-hup! Heave-hup!
  Heave-hup!

THE BIRD. The bird flew down and put his head through the
  hole in the middle,

THE MILLER'S SECOND APPRENTICE. and wearing it like a collar he flew back up to the tree and sang again:

THE BIRD.
'My mother cut my head off,
My father swallowed me,
My sister buried all my bones
Under the juniper tree.
Keewitt! Keewitt! You'll never find
A prettier bird than me!'

THE MILLER'S SECOND APPRENTICE. When he'd finished the song he spread his wings and flew up in the air.

THE MILLER'S FIRST APPRENTICE. In his right claw he had the golden chain,

THE MILLER'S THIRD APPRENTICE. in his left claw he had the shoes,

THE MILLER'S SECOND APPRENTICE. and around his neck was the millstone.

THE BIRD. He flew and he flew all the way back to his father's house.

THE FIRST WIFE. Inside the house,

THE RICH MAN. Father

THE SECOND WIFE. and Mother

MARLEENKEN. and Marleenken

THE RICH MAN. were sitting at the table.

THE FIRST WIFE. Father said,

THE RICH MAN. 'You know, I feel happy for some reason. I feel better than I've done for days.'

THE SECOND WIFE. 'It's all very well for you. I don't feel well at all. I feel as if a bad storm were coming.'

THE FIRST WIFE. As for Marleenken,

MARLEENKEN. she just sat and wept.

THE BIRD. At that moment, the bird arrived. He flew around the house and settled on the roof,

THE FIRST WIFE. and as he did that, Father said,

THE RICH MAN. 'No, I don't think I've ever felt so well.
The sun's shining outside, and I feel as if I'm going to see
an old friend.'

THE SECOND WIFE. 'Well, I feel terrible! I don't know
what's the matter with me. I feel cold and hot all over. My
teeth are chattering and my veins are filled with fire.'

THE FIRST WIFE. She tore open her bodice with
trembling hands.

MARLEENKEN. Marleenken sat in the corner, weeping
and weeping so much that her handkerchief was soaked
right through.

THE RICH MAN. Then the bird left the roof and flew to the
juniper tree, where they could all see him, and he sang:

THE BIRD.
'My mother cut my head off – '

THE FIRST WIFE. The mother pressed her hands over her ears
and squeezed her eyes tight shut.

THE SECOND WIFE. There was a roaring in her head, and
behind her eyelids lightning burned and flashed.

THE BIRD.
'My father swallowed me – '

THE RICH MAN. 'Wife, look at this! You've never seen such a
lovely bird! He's singing like an angel, and the sun's shining
so warmly, and the air smells like cinnamon!'

THE BIRD.
'My sister buried all my bones – '

THE FIRST WIFE. Marleenken laid her head on her knees

MARLEENKEN. sobbing and crying,

THE FIRST WIFE. but the father said,

THE RICH MAN. 'I'm going out. I've got to see this bird
close to!'

THE SECOND WIFE. 'No! Don't go! I feel as if the whole
house is shaking and burning!'

THE RICH MAN. But the father ran out into the sunshine and gazed up at the bird as he sang:

THE BIRD.
 'Under the juniper tree.
 Keewitt! Keewitt! You'll never find
 A prettier bird than me!'

MARLEENKEN. As he sang the last note he dropped the golden chain,

THE RICH MAN. and it fell around the father's neck and fitted him as if it had been made for him.

THE FIRST WIFE. The father ran in at once, and said,

THE RICH MAN. 'What a beautiful bird! And see what he's given me – look!'

THE SECOND WIFE. The woman was too terrified to look.

THE FIRST WIFE. She fell down on the floor, and her cap fell off her head and rolled away into the corner.

THE RICH MAN. Then the bird sang once more:

THE BIRD.
 'My mother cut my head off – '

THE SECOND WIFE. 'No! I can't bear it! I wish I were a thousand feet under the ground, so I wouldn't have to hear that song!'

THE BIRD.
 'My father swallowed me – '

THE FIRST WIFE. And the wife fell down again as if she'd been stunned, and her fingernails were scratching at the floor.

THE BIRD.
 'My sister buried all my bones – '

THE FIRST WIFE. And Marleenken wiped her eyes and got up.

MARLEENKEN. 'I'll go and see if the bird will give me something,'

THE FIRST WIFE. she said, and ran outside.

THE BIRD.
'Under the juniper tree – '

THE RICH MAN. As he said that, the bird threw down the little red shoes.

THE BIRD.
'Keewitt! Keewitt! You'll never find
A prettier bird than me!'

THE FIRST WIFE. Marleenken put on the shoes, and found they fitted her perfectly.

MARLEENKEN. She was delighted,

THE RICH MAN. and she danced and skipped into the house and said,

MARLEENKEN. 'Oh, what a beautiful bird! I was so sad when I went out, and see what he's given me! Mama, look at these lovely shoes!'

THE SECOND WIFE. 'No! No!'

THE RICH MAN. She jumped to her feet, and her hair stood out all round her head like flames of fire.

THE SECOND WIFE. 'I can't stand any more! I feel as if the world were coming to an end! I can't stand it!'

MARLEENKEN. And she ran out of the door and out on to the grass, and

THE SECOND WIFE. – *bam*!

THE BIRD. The bird dropped the millstone on her head, and she was crushed to death.

THE RICH MAN. The father and Marleenken heard the crash

MARLEENKEN. and ran out.

THE RICH MAN. Smoke and flames and fire were rising from the spot,

MARLEENKEN. and then came a breath of wind and cleared them all away;

THE RICH MAN. and when they were gone,

MARLEENKEN. there was little brother standing there.

THE SON. And he took his father by one hand and Marleenken by the other,

THE FIRST WIFE. and all three of them were very happy;

THE RICH MAN. and so they went inside their house

MARLEENKEN. and sat down at the table

THE SON. and ate their supper.

And now, at last, THE FIRST WIFE *is able to rest in peace. She leaves her family, humming the tune to 'Under the Juniper Tree'.*

THE SECOND SET OF TALES

The Frog King, or Iron Heinrich
The Three Little Men in the Woods
Thousandfurs
The Goose Girl at the Spring
Hansel and Gretel
Faithful Johannes

And the one that got away…

The Donkey Cabbage

The Storytellers

The Frog King, or Iron Heinrich

THE KING
THE PRINCESS
THE FROG, *later* THE PRINCE
IRON HEINRICH, *referred to as* FAITHFUL HEINRICH
THE BLACKSMITH

This Tale can be told by a cast of four:
The King / The Blacksmith
The Princess
The Frog, *later* The Prince
Faithful Heinrich

The Three Little Men in the Woods

THE MAN
THE WOMAN, *later* THE STEPMOTHER
THE MAN'S DAUGHTER, *later* THE QUEEN
    and THE WHITE DUCK
THE WOMAN'S DAUGHTER, *later* THE STEPSISTER
THE FIRST LITTLE MAN
THE SECOND LITTLE MAN
THE THIRD LITTLE MAN
THE KING
THE KITCHEN BOY
A COACHMAN

This Tale can be told by a cast of six:
The Man / The First Little Man (*puppet*)
The Woman, *later* The Stepmother / The Second Little Man
    (*puppet*)
The Man's Daughter, *later* The Queen *and* The White Duck
The Woman's Daughter, *later* The Stepsister

The King / The Third Little Man (*puppet*)
The Kitchen Boy / A Coachman

Thousandfurs

THE KING
THE QUEEN
THE FIRST COUNCILLOR
THE SECOND COUNCILLOR
THE THIRD COUNCILLOR
THOUSANDFURS
A WEAVER
A DESIGNER
A HUNTSMAN
A LEATHER WORKER
THE SECOND KING
THE FIRST HUNTSMAN
THE SECOND HUNTSMAN
THE THIRD HUNTSMAN
THREE HOUNDS
THE COOK
THE FIRST SERVANT
THE SECOND SERVANT
THE THIRD SERVANT
THE FIRST BALLGOER
THE SECOND BALLGOER
THE THIRD BALLGOER
THE FOURTH BALLGOER

This Tale can be told by a cast of six:
The King / The Cook / The Fourth Ballgoer
The Queen / Thousandfurs
The Second King / A Huntsman
The Third Councillor / A Leather Worker / Hound (*puppet*) /
    The First Huntsman / The Second Servant / The First Ballgoer
The First Councillor / A Designer / Hound (*puppet*) /
    The Second Huntsman / The Third Servant /
    The Second Ballgoer
The Second Councillor / A Weaver / Hound (*puppet*) /
    The Third Huntsman / The First Servant / The Third Ballgoer

The Goose Girl at the Spring

THE OLD WOMAN
THE GOOSE GIRL
A LITTLE BOY
A FATHER
THE YOUNG COUNT
THE KING
THE QUEEN
THE FIRST BODYGUARD
THE SECOND BODYGUARD
THE OWL

This Tale can be told by a cast of five:
The Old Woman / The Second Bodyguard
The Young Count
The Goose Girl / The First Bodyguard
A Father / The King / The Owl (*puppet*)
A Little Boy (*puppet*) / The Queen

Hansel and Gretel

HANSEL
GRETEL
THE WOODCUTTER
THE STEPMOTHER
THE SNOW-WHITE BIRD
THE WITCH, *initially disguised as* THE OLD WOMAN
THE WHITE DUCK

This Tale can be told by a cast of five:
Hansel
Gretel
The Woodcutter / The Snow-white Bird (*puppet*)
The Stepmother
The Witch / The White Duck (*puppet*)

Faithful Johannes

THE OLD KING
FAITHFUL JOHANNES
THE YOUNG KING
THE FIRST SERVANT
THE SECOND SERVANT
THE THIRD SERVANT
THE FOURTH SERVANT
THE FIRST GOLDSMITH
THE SECOND GOLDSMITH
THE THIRD GOLDSMITH
A SAILOR
THE BOSUN
THE CHAMBERMAID
THE PRINCESS OF THE GOLDEN ROOF,
    later THE QUEEN
THE FIRST RAVEN
THE SECOND RAVEN
THE THIRD RAVEN
THE PRIEST
THE HANGMAN
THE FIRST PRINCE
THE SECOND PRINCE

This Tale can be told by a cast of six:
Faithful Johannes
The Young King
The Princess of the Golden Roof, *later* The Queen /
    The Fourth Servant
The Old King / The Third Goldsmith / The Bosun /
    The First Raven / The Third Servant / The Priest
The Second Servant / The First Goldsmith / The Chambermaid /
    The Second Raven / The First Prince (*puppet*)
The First Servant / The Second Goldsmith / A Sailor / The Third
    Raven / The Hangman / The Second Prince (*puppet*)

The Donkey Cabbage

THE YOUNG HUNTER
AN OLD WOMAN
THE HUNTER'S MOTHER
THE HUNTER'S FATHER
THE WITCH
THE DAUGHTER
THE FIRST GIANT
THE SECOND GIANT
THE THIRD GIANT
THE SERVING GIRL
THE MILLER

This Tale can be told by a cast of five:
The Young Hunter
An Old Woman / The Witch
The Hunter's Mother / The Second Giant / The Serving Girl
The Hunter's Father / The First Giant / The Miller
The Daughter / The Third Giant

The Frog King, or Iron Heinrich

For this Tale, two locations in THE KING*'s palace are needed –
the dining room and* THE PRINCESS*'s bedchamber. For both of
these, doors are important. Outside, there's the carriageway…
and, of course, the place in the deep dark forest where, under a
lime tree, there is a well. There are many ways to depict a frog:
whichever you chose, his moment of transformation is critical.*

You might like to consider a prologue, in which we see how
THE PRINCE *upset the Witch, and how she put a curse on
him. Or you may prefer to keep the surprise, for when the spell
is broken.*

FAITHFUL HEINRICH. In the olden days,

THE FROG. when wishing still worked,

THE KING. there lived a king whose daughters were all
beautiful;

THE PRINCESS. but the youngest daughter

THE KING. was so lovely that even the sun, who has seen
many things, was struck with wonder every time he shone
on her face.

FAITHFUL HEINRICH. Not far away from the king's palace
there was a deep dark forest,

THE FROG. and under a lime tree in the forest there was a well.

THE KING. In the heat of the day the princess used to go into
the forest and sit by the edge of the well,

THE PRINCESS. from which a marvellous coolness seemed
to flow.

THE KING. To pass the time she had a golden ball, which she
used to throw up in the air and catch.

THE PRINCESS. It was her favourite game.

THE KING. Now one day it happened that she threw it a little
carelessly, and she couldn't catch it.

FAITHFUL HEINRICH. Instead the ball rolled away from her

THE FROG. and towards the well,

THE PRINCESS. and then it ran right over the edge and
disappeared.

A moment of shock: it's lost!

THE KING. The princess ran after it, and looked down into
the water;

THE PRINCESS. but it was so deep that she couldn't see the
ball. She couldn't even see the bottom of the well.

FAITHFUL HEINRICH. She began to cry, and she cried louder
and louder, inconsolably.

THE KING. But as she wept and sobbed, someone spoke to her.

THE FROG (*just his disembodied voice*). 'What's the matter,
princess? You're crying so bitterly, you'd move a stone
to pity.'

FAITHFUL HEINRICH. She looked round to see where the
voice was coming from,

THE KING. and saw a frog who'd stuck his big ugly head out
of the water.

And THE FROG *appears*.

THE PRINCESS. 'Oh, it's you, you old splasher. I'm crying
because my golden ball's fallen into the water and it's so
deep and I can't see it.'

THE FROG. 'Well, you can stop crying now. I can help you,
but what will you give me if I fetch your ball for you?'

THE PRINCESS. 'Whatever you want, frog! Anything!
My clothes, my pearls, my jewels, even the golden crown
I'm wearing.'

THE FROG 'I don't want your clothes, and your jewels and
your golden crown are no good to me, but if you love me and
take me as your companion and your playmate, if you let me

sit next to you at the table and eat from your dish and drink from your cup and sleep in your bed, then I'll dive down and bring up your golden ball.'

FAITHFUL HEINRICH. The princess thought,

THE PRINCESS. 'What is this stupid frog saying? Whatever he thinks, he'll have to stay in the water where he belongs. Perhaps he can get my ball.'

THE KING. But of course she didn't say that.

FAITHFUL HEINRICH. Instead she said,

THE PRINCESS. 'Yes, yes, I'll promise you all of that if you just bring me my ball.'

THE KING. As soon as the frog heard her say 'Yes', he put his head under the water and dived to the bottom.

FAITHFUL HEINRICH. A moment later he came swimming back up with the ball in his mouth, and he threw it on to the grass.

THE KING. The princess was so happy to see it that she snatched it up and ran off at once.

THE FROG. 'Wait, wait!'

FAITHFUL HEINRICH. called the frog.

THE FROG. 'Take me with you! I can't hop as fast as you can run!'

THE PRINCESS. But she took no notice.

THE KING. She hurried home

And THE PRINCESS *slams the palace door shut.*

FAITHFUL HEINRICH. and forgot all about the poor frog,

THE FROG. who had to go back down into his well.

THE KING. Next day the princess was sitting at table with her father the king

FAITHFUL HEINRICH. and all the people of the court, and eating off her golden plate,

THE PRINCESS. when something came hopping up the marble steps:

FAITHFUL HEINRICH. plip plop,

THE PRINCESS. plip plop.

THE KING. When it reached the top – (*Knock knock.*) it knocked at the door and called:

THE FROG. 'Princess! Youngest princess! Open the door for me!'

FAITHFUL HEINRICH. She ran to see who it was, and opened the door,

THE PRINCESS. and there was the frog.

THE KING. Frightened – (*Slam.*) she slammed the door shut at once and ran back to the table.

FAITHFUL HEINRICH. The king saw that her heart was pounding, and said,

THE KING. 'What are you afraid of, my child? Is there a giant there at the door?'

THE PRINCESS. 'Oh, no, it's not a giant, it's a horrible frog.'

THE KING. 'What does the frog want with you?'

THE PRINCESS. 'Oh, Papa, yesterday when I was playing in the forest near the well, my golden ball fell in the water. And I started to cry and because I was crying so much, the frog got it for me, and because he insisted, I had to promise that he could be my companion. But I didn't think he'd ever leave the water, not really. But there he is outside the door and he wants to come in!'

FAITHFUL HEINRICH. And then there came – (*Knock knock knock.*) a second knock at the door, and a voice called:

THE FROG.
'Princess, princess, youngest daughter,
Open up and let me in!
Or else your promise by the water
Isn't worth a rusty pin.

Keep your promise, royal daughter,
Open up and let me in!'

FAITHFUL HEINRICH. The king said,

THE KING. 'If you make a promise, you have to keep it.
Go and let him in.'

FAITHFUL HEINRICH. She opened the door

THE PRINCESS. and the frog hopped in. He hopped all the
way to her chair.

THE FROG. 'Lift me up. I want to sit next to you.'

THE PRINCESS. She didn't want to,

FAITHFUL HEINRICH. but the king said,

THE KING. 'Go on. Do as he says.'

THE PRINCESS. So she lifted the frog up.

THE KING. Once he was on the chair, he wanted to be on
the table,

THE PRINCESS. so she had to lift him up there as well,

FAITHFUL HEINRICH. and then he said,

THE FROG. 'Push your golden plate a bit closer so I can eat
with you.'

THE KING. She did, but everyone could see that she wasn't
enjoying it.

THE FROG. The frog was, though; he ate her food with
great pleasure,

THE PRINCESS. while every mouthful seemed to stick in the
princess's throat.

FAITHFUL HEINRICH. Finally the frog said,

THE FROG. 'Well, I've had enough now, thank you, I'd like to
go to bed. Carry me up to your room and get your silken bed
ready so we can sleep in it.'

THE KING. The princess began to cry,

THE PRINCESS. because the frog's cold skin frightened her.
She trembled at the thought of him in her sweet clean bed.

FAITHFUL HEINRICH. But the king frowned and said,

THE KING. 'You shouldn't despise someone who helped you when you were in trouble!'

THE PRINCESS. She picked the frog up between finger and thumb and set him down outside her bedroom door – (*Slam.*) and shut it firmly.

Knock... knock... knock...

FAITHFUL HEINRICH. But he kept on knocking and called,

THE FROG (*knock*). 'Let me in! (*Knock.*) Let me in!'

FAITHFUL HEINRICH. So she opened the door and said,

THE PRINCESS. 'All right! You can come in, but you must sleep on the floor.'

THE KING. She made him lie down at the foot of her bed. But still he said,

THE FROG. 'Let me up! Let me up! I'm just as tired as you.'

THE PRINCESS. 'Oh, for goodness' sake!'

FAITHFUL HEINRICH. she said,

THE KING. and picked him up

THE PRINCESS. and put him at the far end of her pillow.

THE FROG. 'Closer! Closer!'

THE PRINCESS. But that was too much.

FAITHFUL HEINRICH. In a flash of anger she scooped up the frog

THE KING. and threw him against the wall.

Suddenly, surprisingly, violently, THE FROG *is transformed.*

FAITHFUL HEINRICH. But when he fell back into the bed,

THE KING. what a surprise!

THE PRINCESS. He wasn't a frog any more.

FAITHFUL HEINRICH. In fact he'd become a young man –

THE PRINCE. a prince –

THE PRINCESS. with beautiful smiling eyes. And she
loved him

And they kiss.

THE PRINCE. and accepted him as her companion,

THE KING. just as the king would have wished.

THE PRINCE. The prince told her that an evil witch had put
a spell on him,

THE PRINCESS. and that only she, the princess, could have
rescued him from the well.

FAITHFUL HEINRICH. What's more, on the following day
a carriage would come to take them to the prince's kingdom.

THE PRINCE. Then they fell asleep

THE PRINCESS. side by side.

*A moment of peace – and then the palace bursts into
life again.*

THE KING. And next morning no sooner had the sun
awoken them

THE PRINCESS. than a carriage drew up outside the palace,

THE PRINCE. just as the prince had said.

THE KING. It was pulled by eight horses

THE PRINCESS. with ostrich plumes nodding on their heads
and golden chains shining among their harness.

FAITHFUL HEINRICH. At the back of the coach was
Faithful Heinrich.

THE PRINCE. He was the prince's servant,

THE BLACKSMITH. and when he'd learned that his master
had been changed into a frog,

FAITHFUL HEINRICH. he was so dismayed that he went
straight to the blacksmith and ordered three iron bands to put
around his heart to stop it bursting with grief.

And THE BLACKSMITH *hammers these bands shut: clink, clink, clink.*

THE PRINCESS. Faithful Heinrich helped them into the carriage

THE KING. and took his place at the back.

FAITHFUL HEINRICH. He was overjoyed to see the prince again.

THE KING. When they'd gone a little way – (*Crack!*) the prince heard a loud crack from behind. He turned around and called out:

THE PRINCE. 'Heinrich, the coach is breaking!'

FAITHFUL HEINRICH. 'No, no, my lord, it's just my heart. When you were living in the well, when you were a frog, I suffered such great pain that I bound my heart with iron bands to stop it breaking, for iron is stronger than grief. But love is stronger than iron, and now you're human again the iron bands are falling off.'

THE PRINCE. And twice more they heard the same cracking noise – (*Crack!*)

THE PRINCESS. and each time they thought it was the carriage – (*Crack!*)

FAITHFUL HEINRICH. but each time they were wrong:

THE KING. it was an iron band breaking away from Faithful Heinrich's heart,

FAITHFUL HEINRICH. because his master was safe again.

The Three Little Men in the Woods

This Tale is another one that has many locations. The major challenges are the depiction of THE THREE LITTLE MEN (*in the original production, these were puppets*) *and the vomiting coins and frogs* (*look online for coins-from-mouth magic tricks*).

THE KITCHEN BOY. Once

THE MAN. there was a man whose wife died,

THE WOMAN. and a woman whose husband died;

THE MAN'S DAUGHTER. and the man had a daughter,

THE WOMAN'S DAUGHTER. and so did the woman.

THE KING. The girls knew each other,

THE WOMAN'S DAUGHTER. and one day they went for a walk together,

THE MAN'S DAUGHTER. and they came to the woman's house.

THE KITCHEN BOY. The woman took the man's daughter aside, and when her own daughter wasn't listening, she said,

THE WOMAN. 'You know, I'd like to marry your father. Tell him that, and see what he says. If he says yes, I promise you'll have milk to wash your face in every day, it's very good for your complexion, and wine to drink. And my daughter will only have water. That's how much I'd like to marry him.'

THE MAN'S DAUGHTER. The girl went home and told her father what the woman had said.

THE KING. The man said,

THE MAN. 'Marry her? Oh, good grief. What shall I do? Marriage is delightful, but it can be a torment as well, you know.'

THE WOMAN. He couldn't make up his mind.

THE WOMAN'S DAUGHTER. Finally, he pulled off his boot and said to his daughter,

THE MAN. 'Here, take this boot. It's got a hole in the sole. Hang it up in the attic, and then fill it up with water. If it holds the water, I'll take a wife, but if the water runs away then I won't.'

THE KITCHEN BOY. The girl did as she was told.

THE MAN'S DAUGHTER. The water made the leather swell and squeeze the hole shut, so that when she filled up the boot, all the water stayed in it.

THE KING. The girl told her father,

THE KITCHEN BOY. and he went up to the attic to see.

THE MAN. 'Well, fancy that! I shall have to marry her, then. You can't go back once you've made a vow.'

THE MAN'S DAUGHTER. He put his best suit on

THE MAN. and went to woo the widow,

THE WOMAN. and presently they were married.

There follows a sequence of diminishing returns, with
THE WOMAN *swapping round the milk, wine and water,*
like a magician's three-cup shuffle.

THE KITCHEN BOY. Next morning when the two girls got up,

THE MAN'S DAUGHTER. the man's daughter found there was milk for her to wash her face in and wine for her to drink.

THE WOMAN'S DAUGHTER. The woman's daughter only had water.

THE KING. On the second morning,

THE WOMAN'S DAUGHTER. both girls had water for washing

THE MAN'S DAUGHTER. and water to drink.

THE KITCHEN BOY. On the third morning,

THE MAN'S DAUGHTER. the man's daughter had water,

THE WOMAN'S DAUGHTER. but the woman's daughter had milk to wash in

THE STEPMOTHER. and wine to drink,

THE MAN'S DAUGHTER. and so it was on every morning after that.

THE KING. The fact was that the woman hated her stepdaughter,

THE STEPMOTHER. and every day she thought of new ways to torment her.

THE KITCHEN BOY. At the root of her hatred was bitter envy,

THE KING. because her stepdaughter was beautiful and sweet-tempered,

THE KITCHEN BOY. whereas her own daughter was ugly and selfish,

THE STEPMOTHER. and not even full-cream milk made her complexion any nicer.

THE MAN. One winter's day,

THE KING. when everything was frozen hard,

THE STEPSISTER. the woman made a dress out of paper.

THE KITCHEN BOY. She called her stepdaughter and said,

THE STEPMOTHER. 'Here, put this on. Then go into the woods and gather some strawberries for me. I want some, and nothing else will do.'

THE MAN'S DAUGHTER. 'But strawberries don't grow in the winter. Everything's covered in snow, and the ground's as hard as iron. And why must I wear this dress made of paper? The wind will blow through it, and the brambles will tear it to pieces.'

THE STEPMOTHER. 'Don't you dare argue with me! Be on your way, and don't come back till you've filled the basket with strawberries.'

THE KITCHEN BOY. Then she gave the girl a piece of bread as hard as wood.

THE STEPMOTHER. 'Here's your food. You'll have to make it last all day, we're not made of money.'

THE STEPSISTER. Secretly she thought,

THE STEPMOTHER. 'If the cold doesn't kill her, the hunger will, and I'll never have to see her again.'

THE MAN. The girl did as she was told.

THE KING. She put on the flimsy paper dress

THE KITCHEN BOY. and went out with the basket.

THE STEPSISTER. Of course there was snow everywhere, with not a green leaf to be seen,

THE MAN'S DAUGHTER. far less a strawberry.

THE KITCHEN BOY. She didn't know where to look,

THE STEPSISTER. so she went into the woods along a path she didn't know,

THE KITCHEN BOY. and soon she came to a little house that was about as high as her head.

THE MAN'S DAUGHTER. Sitting on a bench outside it smoking their pipes were three little men, each about as tall as her knee,

THE KITCHEN BOY. as she saw when they all got up and bowed.

THE MAN'S DAUGHTER. 'Good morning,'

THE KITCHEN BOY. she said.

THE FIRST LITTLE MAN. 'What a nice girl!' one of them said.

THE SECOND LITTLE MAN. 'Well mannered,' said a second.

THE THIRD LITTLE MAN. 'Ask her in,' said the third. 'It's cold.'

THE FIRST LITTLE MAN. 'She's wearing paper,' said the first.

THE SECOND LITTLE MAN. 'Fashionable, I expect,' said
the second.

THE THIRD LITTLE MAN. 'Chilly, though,' said the third.

THE THREE LITTLE MEN. 'Would you like to come inside,
miss?' they all said together.

THE MAN'S DAUGHTER. 'How kind of you. Yes, I would.'

THE KITCHEN BOY. They knocked out their pipes before
opening the door.

THE FIRST LITTLE MAN. 'Mustn't smoke near paper,'
said one.

THE SECOND LITTLE MAN. 'Catch fire in a moment,' said
the second.

THE THIRD LITTLE MAN. 'Terrible danger,' said the third.

THE STEPSISTER. They gave her a little chair to sit on,

THE MAN'S DAUGHTER. and all three of them sat on a
bench next to the fire.

THE KITCHEN BOY. She felt hungry, so she took out her
piece of bread.

THE MAN'S DAUGHTER. 'Do you mind if I eat my breakfast?'

THE FIRST LITTLE MAN. 'What is it?'

THE MAN'S DAUGHTER. 'Just a piece of bread.'

THE SECOND LITTLE MAN. 'Can we have a bit?'

THE MAN'S DAUGHTER. 'Of course,'

THE KITCHEN BOY. she said,

THE THIRD LITTLE MAN. and broke it in two.

THE STEPSISTER. It was so hard she had to knock it on the
edge of the little table.

THE KITCHEN BOY. She gave the little men the bigger bit,
and started to gnaw the smaller one.

THE THIRD LITTLE MAN.
  'What are you doing

THE SECOND LITTLE MAN.
                    out here

THE FIRST LITTLE MAN.
                        in the wild woods?'

THE THREE LITTLE MEN. they said.

THE MAN'S DAUGHTER. 'I'm supposed to gather
  strawberries. I don't know where I'm going to find any,
  but I'm not allowed to go home till I've filled my basket.'

THE THIRD LITTLE MAN. The first little man whispered
  something to the second,

THE FIRST LITTLE MAN. and the second whispered to
  the third,

THE SECOND LITTLE MAN. and then the third whispered
  to the first.

THE MAN'S DAUGHTER. Then they all looked at her.

THE FIRST *and* THE THIRD LITTLE MAN. 'Will you sweep
  the path for us?'

THE SECOND LITTLE MAN. they said. 'There's a broom in
  the corner.

THE THIRD LITTLE MAN. Just clear the path a bit next to the
  back door.'

THE MAN'S DAUGHTER . 'Yes, I'd be glad to,'

THE KITCHEN BOY. she said,

THE STEPSISTER. and she took the broom and went out.

THE KITCHEN BOY. When she'd gone they said,

THE THREE LITTLE MEN. 'What shall we give her?

THE FIRST LITTLE MAN. Such a polite girl.

THE SECOND LITTLE MAN. Shared her bread with us,

THE THIRD LITTLE MAN. and it was all she had!

THE FIRST LITTLE MAN. Gave us the biggest bit!

THE SECOND LITTLE MAN. Kindly as well as polite.

THE THIRD LITTLE MAN. What shall we give her?'

THE KITCHEN BOY. And the first one said,

THE FIRST LITTLE MAN. 'I'll make sure she grows more and more beautiful each day.'

THE KITCHEN BOY. The second one said,

THE SECOND LITTLE MAN. 'I'll make sure that every time she speaks, a gold piece will fall from her mouth.'

THE KITCHEN BOY. The third one said,

THE THIRD LITTLE MAN. 'I'll make sure that a king will come along and marry her.'

THE STEPSISTER. Meanwhile, the girl was brushing away the snow from the path,

THE KITCHEN BOY. and what did she find there but

THE MAN'S DAUGHTER. strawberries, dozens of them, as red and ripe as if it were summer.

THE STEPSISTER. She looked back at the house,

THE MAN'S DAUGHTER. and she saw the three little men all looking from the back window.

THE FIRST LITTLE MAN. Yes, they nodded,

THE SECOND LITTLE MAN. go ahead,

THE THIRD LITTLE MAN. pick as many as you want.

THE KITCHEN BOY. She filled the basket, and went to thank the little men.

THE MAN'S DAUGHTER. They all lined up to bow and shake her hand.

THE SECOND LITTLE MAN. 'Goodbye!

THE THIRD LITTLE MAN. Goodbye!

THE FIRST LITTLE MAN. Goodbye!'

THE FIRST LITTLE MAN *follows* THE MAN'S
DAUGHTER *and, from here on, comments on the action,
as the* THREE LITTLE MEN*'s predictions are fulfilled.*

THE FIRST LITTLE MAN. She went home and gave the
basket to her stepmother.

THE STEPMOTHER. 'Where did you get these?'

THE KITCHEN BOY. the woman snapped.

THE MAN'S DAUGHTER. 'I found a little house – '

THE KITCHEN BOY. she began,

Just then, she coughs up – a coin!

THE STEPSISTER. but a gold piece fell out of her mouth.

THE STEPMOTHER. As she continued to speak,

THE MAN'S DAUGHTER *opens her mouth, and another
coin comes out.*

THE KING. more and more gold pieces fell to the floor – (*Coin.*)

THE KITCHEN BOY. till they were heaped around her ankles.
(*A pile of coins.*)

THE STEPSISTER. 'Look at her showing off! I could do that if
I wanted. It's not that clever.'

THE KING. Of course, the stepsister was really wild with envy,

THE KITCHEN BOY. and as soon as they were alone she said
to her mother:

THE STEPSISTER. 'Let me go to the woods and pick
strawberries! I want to! I really want to!'

THE STEPMOTHER. 'No, darling, it's too cold. You could
freeze to death.'

THE STEPSISTER. 'Oh, go on! Please! I'll give you half the
gold coins that fall out of my mouth! Go on!'

THE STEPMOTHER. Finally the mother gave in.

THE FIRST LITTLE MAN. She took her best fur coat and
altered it so it fitted the girl,

THE KING. and gave her chicken-liver pâté sandwiches

THE STEPSISTER. and a big piece of chocolate cake for
the journey.

THE MAN'S DAUGHTER. The stepsister went into the woods
and found the little house.

THE FIRST LITTLE MAN. The three little men were inside,

THE SECOND LITTLE MAN. looking through the window,

THE THIRD LITTLE MAN. but she didn't see them,

THE MAN'S DAUGHTER. and she opened the door and went
straight in.

THE STEPSISTER. 'Move out the way. I want to sit next to
the fire.'

THE KITCHEN BOY. The three little men sat on their bench and
watched as she took out her chicken-liver pâté sandwiches.

THE THREE LITTLE MEN. 'What's that?' they said.

THE STEPSISTER. 'My lunch,'

THE MAN'S DAUGHTER. she said with her mouth full.

THE SECOND LITTLE MAN. 'Can we have some?'

THE STEPSISTER. 'Certainly not.'

THE THIRD LITTLE MAN. 'What about that cake? It's a big
piece. Do you want all of it?'

THE STEPSISTER. 'There's hardly enough for me. Get your
own cake.'

THE MAN'S DAUGHTER. When she'd finished eating
they said,

THE THREE LITTLE MAN. 'You can sweep the path now.'

THE STEPSISTER. 'I'm not sweeping any path. D'you think
I'm your servant? What a nerve.'

THE MAN'S DAUGHTER. They just smoked their pipes and
looked at her,

THE KITCHEN BOY. and since they obviously weren't going
to give her anything,

THE STEPSISTER. she left and looked around for strawberries.

THE FIRST LITTLE MAN. 'What a rude girl!' said the first
little man.

THE SECOND LITTLE MAN. 'Selfish, too,' said the second.

THE THIRD LITTLE MAN. 'Not as good as the last one, by
a long way,' said the third.

THE THREE LITTLE MEN. 'What shall we give *her*?'

THE FIRST LITTLE MAN. 'I'll make sure that she gets uglier
every day.'

THE SECOND LITTLE MAN. 'I'll make sure that every time
she speaks, a toad jumps out of her mouth.'

THE THIRD LITTLE MAN. 'I'll make sure she dies an
uncomfortable death.'

THE MAN'S DAUGHTER. The girl couldn't find any
strawberries,

THE STEPSISTER. so she went home to complain.

As she finishes speaking, she coughs up – a toad!

THE FIRST LITTLE MAN. Every time she opened her mouth
(*Toad.*) a toad jumped out – (*Toad.*)

THE KING. and soon the floor was covered in the crawling,
squatting, flopping things – (*A pile of toads.*)

THE STEPMOTHER. and even her mother found her repellent.

THE KING. After that the stepmother became obsessed.

THE FIRST LITTLE MAN. It was as if she had a worm
gnawing in her brain.

THE KITCHEN BOY. The only thing she thought about was
how to make her stepdaughter's life a misery,

THE KING. and to add to her torment,

THE STEPMOTHER. the girl was growing more and more
beautiful each day.

THE FIRST LITTLE MAN. Finally the woman boiled a skein
of yarn and hung it over the girl's shoulder.

THE STEPMOTHER. 'Here, take the axe and go and chop a hole in the ice on the river. Rinse this yarn, and don't take all day about it.'

THE STEPSISTER. She hoped the girl would fall in and drown, of course. (*Burps and then swallows a toad.*)

THE FIRST LITTLE MAN. Her stepdaughter did what she was told. She took the axe and the yarn to the river,

THE MAN'S DAUGHTER. and she was just about to step on to the ice when a passing carriage drew to a halt. (*Coin.*)

A COACHMAN. In the carriage there happened to be a king.

THE KING. 'Stop! What are you doing? That ice isn't safe!'

THE MAN'S DAUGHTER. 'I've got to rinse this yarn' – (*Coin.*)

THE FIRST LITTLE MAN. The king saw how beautiful she was, and opened the carriage door.

THE KING. 'Would you like to come with me?'

THE MAN'S DAUGHTER. 'Yes, I would,'

A COACHMAN. she said,

THE MAN'S DAUGHTER. 'gladly' – (*Coin.*)

THE FIRST LITTLE MAN. because she was happy to get away from the woman and her daughter.

A COACHMAN. So she got in and the carriage drove away.

THE KING. 'Now I happen to be looking for a wife. My advisers have told me it's time I got married. You're not married, are you?'

THE MAN'S DAUGHTER. 'No' – (*Coin.*)

A COACHMAN. said the girl and neatly dropped the gold piece into her pocket.

THE FIRST LITTLE MAN. The king was fascinated.

THE KING. 'What a clever trick! Will you marry me?'

THE MAN'S DAUGHTER. She agreed,

THE KING. and their wedding was celebrated as soon as possible.

THE FIRST LITTLE MAN. So it all came about as the little men had promised.

THE QUEEN. A year later the young queen gave birth

THE KING. to a baby boy.

THE KITCHEN BOY. The whole country rejoiced,

THE STEPSISTER. and it was reported in all the newspapers.

A toad drops out from behind the paper she is holding up.

THE STEPMOTHER. The stepmother heard about it,

THE FIRST LITTLE MAN. and she and her daughter went to the palace,

THE STEPSISTER. pretending to pay the queen a friendly visit. (*Burp.*)

THE KING. The king happened to be out,

THE FIRST LITTLE MAN. and when no one else was around,

THE KITCHEN BOY. the woman and her daughter got hold of the queen

THE FIRST LITTLE MAN. and threw her out of the window into the stream running below,

THE STEPMOTHER. where she drowned at once.

THE STEPSISTER. Her body sank to the bottom and was hidden by the waterweeds. (*Burp.*)

THE STEPMOTHER. 'Now you lie down in her bed,'

THE KITCHEN BOY. the woman said to her daughter.

THE STEPMOTHER. 'Don't say anything, whatever you do.'

THE STEPSISTER. 'Why not?' (*Toad.*)

THE STEPMOTHER. 'Toads,'

THE KITCHEN BOY. said the woman,

THE STEPMOTHER. picking up the one that had just jumped out,

THE KITCHEN BOY. and throwing it out of the window after the queen.

THE STEPMOTHER. 'Now just lie there. Do as I say.'

THE KITCHEN BOY. The woman covered her daughter's head, because quite apart from the toads she had indeed grown even uglier every day.

THE FIRST LITTLE MAN. When the king came back, the woman explained that the queen had a fever.

THE STEPMOTHER. 'She must be quiet. No conversation. Mustn't speak at all. You must let her rest.'

THE FIRST LITTLE MAN. The king murmured some tender words to the daughter under the blankets, and left.

THE KING. Next morning he came to see her again,

THE STEPMOTHER. and before the woman could stop her,

THE STEPSISTER. the daughter answered him when he spoke. (*Toad.*)

THE KITCHEN BOY. Out jumped a toad.

THE KING. 'Good Lord – what's that?'

THE STEPSISTER. 'I can't help it' – (*Toad.*)

THE FIRST LITTLE MAN. said the daughter, as another toad came out,

THE STEPSISTER. 'it's not my fault' – (*Toad.*)

THE KITCHEN BOY. and another.

THE KING. 'What's going on? Whatever's the matter?'

THE STEPMOTHER. 'She's got toad flu. It's very infectious. But she'll soon get over it, as long as she's not disturbed.'

THE KING. 'I do hope so.'

And he leaves them, troubled.

THE FIRST LITTLE MAN. That night, the kitchen boy was wiping the last of the pots and pans

THE KITCHEN BOY. when he saw a white duck swimming up the drain that led out of the scullery into the stream.

A figure (the ghost of THE QUEEN) *appears, veiled in white, carrying in front of her* THE WHITE DUCK.

THE FIRST LITTLE MAN. The duck said:

THE WHITE DUCK. 'The king's asleep, and I must weep.'

THE KITCHEN BOY. The kitchen boy didn't know what to say.

THE FIRST LITTLE MAN. Then the duck spoke again:

THE WHITE DUCK. 'And what of my guests?'

THE KITCHEN BOY. 'They're taking their rest.'

THE WHITE DUCK. 'And my sweet little baby?'

THE KITCHEN BOY. 'He's sleeping too, maybe.'

THE FIRST LITTLE MAN. Then the duck shimmered and her form changed into that of the queen.

Secretly, THE KITCHEN BOY *follows her.*

THE KITCHEN BOY. She went upstairs to the baby's cradle,

THE QUEEN'S GHOST. and took him out and nursed him,

THE KITCHEN BOY. and then she laid him down tenderly and tucked him in and kissed him.

THE FIRST LITTLE MAN. Finally she floated back to the kitchen,

THE KITCHEN BOY. changed back into the form of the duck,

THE WHITE DUCK. and swam down the gutter and back to the stream.

THE FIRST LITTLE MAN. The kitchen boy had followed her,

THE KITCHEN BOY. and seen everything.

THE FIRST LITTLE MAN. Next night she came again,

THE KITCHEN BOY. and the same thing happened.

THE FIRST LITTLE MAN. On the third night, the ghost said
to the boy:

THE QUEEN'S GHOST. 'Go and tell the king what you've
seen. Tell him to bring his sword and pass it over my head
three times, and then cut my head off.'

THE KITCHEN BOY. The kitchen boy ran to the king

THE KING. and told him everything.

THE KITCHEN BOY. The king was horrified.

THE FIRST LITTLE MAN. He tiptoed into the queen's
bedchamber,

THE KITCHEN BOY. lifted the blankets from her head,

THE FIRST LITTLE MAN. and gasped at the sight of the ugly
daughter lying there

THE KING. snoring,

THE FIRST LITTLE MAN. with a toad for company.

THE KING. 'Take me to the ghost!'

THE FIRST LITTLE MAN. he said, strapping on his sword.

THE KITCHEN BOY. When they got to the kitchen the queen's
ghost stood in front of him,

THE FIRST LITTLE MAN. and the king waved his sword
three times over her head.

THE KITCHEN BOY. At once her form shimmered and
changed into that of the white duck,

THE FIRST LITTLE MAN. and immediately the king swung
his sword

THE KING. and cut her head off.

THE KITCHEN BOY. A moment later the duck vanished,

THE QUEEN. and in her place stood the real queen,

THE KING. alive again.

THE FIRST LITTLE MAN. They greeted each other joyfully.

THE KING. But the king had a plan,

THE QUEEN. And the queen agreed to hide in a different bedchamber till the following Sunday, when the baby was going to be baptised.

THE FIRST LITTLE MAN. At the baptism the false queen stood there heavily veiled,

THE STEPMOTHER. with her mother close, both pretending that she was too ill to speak.

THE FIRST LITTLE MAN. The king said,

THE KING. 'What punishment should someone receive who drags an innocent victim out of bed and throws her into the river to drown?'

THE KITCHEN BOY. The stepmother said at once,

THE STEPMOTHER. 'That's a dreadful crime. The murderer should be put into a barrel studded with nails, and rolled downhill into the water.'

THE KING. 'Then that is what we shall do.'

An ominous drumbeat.

THE FIRST LITTLE MAN. He ordered such a barrel made,

THE KITCHEN BOY. and as soon as it was ready,

THE STEPMOTHER. the woman and her daughter were put inside

THE STEPSISTER. and the top was nailed down.

THE QUEEN. The barrel was rolled downhill till it fell into the river,

THE KING. and that was the end of them.

Thousandfurs

Two palaces feature in this Tale, between which lies a dark forest. Some sleight of hand is required in the design of the dresses, to ensure that THOUSANDFURS' *transformation for the three balls – and speedy return to kitchen maid – is achieved nimbly, yet with appropriate ritual. In the original production, three* STORYTELLERS *assisted with these; each was responsible for one element of the process.*

THE SECOND KING. Once

THE KING. there was a king

THE FIRST COUNCILLOR. whose golden-haired wife was so lovely

THE SECOND COUNCILLOR. that her equal couldn't be found anywhere in the world.

THE QUEEN. It so happened that she fell ill,

THE THIRD COUNCILLOR. and feeling that she was about to die, she said to the king,

THE QUEEN. 'If you marry again when I'm dead, you mustn't marry anyone less beautiful than me, or with hair less golden than mine. You must promise me.'

THE KING. The king gave his promise,

THE FIRST COUNCILLOR. and soon afterwards she closed her eyes and died.

THE SECOND COUNCILLOR. For a long time the king was inconsolable,

THE KING. and couldn't even think about taking a second wife.

THE THIRD COUNCILLOR. But eventually his councillors said,

THE FIRST COUNCILLOR. 'Your majesty, there's no getting away from it:

THE SECOND COUNCILLOR. the country *needs* a queen.

THE THIRD COUNCILLOR. You must marry again.'

THE FIRST COUNCILLOR. So messengers were sent out far and wide to look for a bride as beautiful as the queen had been.

THE SECOND KING. However, they had no success, no matter how far they looked.

THE KING. Besides, even if they had found someone as beautiful, she might not have had golden hair.

THE THIRD COUNCILLOR. The messengers came home empty-handed.

We see THOUSANDFURS *for the first time.*

THE SECOND COUNCILLOR. Now the king had a daughter

THOUSANDFURS. whose hair was as golden as her mother's had been,

THE FIRST COUNCILLOR. During her childhood the king hadn't noticed it,

THE THIRD COUNCILLOR. but one day soon after she came of age he happened to see her as the sun shone through the window on her golden hair.

THE KING. Suddenly he saw that she was as beautiful as her mother had been,

THE FIRST COUNCILLOR. and he fell passionately in love with her on the spot.

THE SECOND KING. He summoned the privy council and announced,

THE KING. 'I have found a bride at last. There is no one in the nation as beautiful as my daughter, so I have determined to marry her.'

THE THIRD COUNCILLOR. The councillors were appalled.

THE FIRST COUNCILLOR. 'Your majesty, this is impossible!

THE SECOND COUNCILLOR. The Lord God has forbidden any such thing!

THE THIRD COUNCILLOR. It is one of the very worst sins.

THE FIRST COUNCILLOR. No good could ever come of it,

THE SECOND COUNCILLOR. and the nation would fall
   into ruin!'

THOUSANDFURS. As for the girl, she was horrified.

THE SECOND KING. Hoping to gain a little time, she said,

THOUSANDFURS. 'Dear Father, before I marry you, I'll need
   three dresses: one as gold as the sun, one as silver as the
   moon and one that glitters like the stars. And what's more
   I must have a cloak made of a thousand different kinds of fur
   – one for every different kind of animal in the kingdom.'

THE SECOND COUNCILLOR. She thought that would be
   impossible, and it would keep him from carrying out his
   wicked plan.

THE KING. But the king was so mad with love that nothing
   would stop him.

   A hive of activity.

A WEAVER. He engaged the most skilful weavers in the land
   to weave three kinds of cloth,

A DESIGNER. and the finest designers to cut it and sew it into
   three magnificent dresses.

A HUNTSMAN. Meanwhile he set his huntsmen to work in
   the forest,

THOUSANDFURS. and day after day they came home with
   their trophies of fur and skin.

A LEATHER WORKER. The best workers in leather and fur
   cut a thousand different pieces and sewed them together,

THOUSANDFURS (*as the three dresses are presented to her*).
   and before long it was clear to the girl that her father was
   going to supply everything she'd asked for.

THE FIRST COUNCILLOR. Then came a day when he said,

THE KING (*slipping the cloak over her shoulders*). 'My
   darling, everything is nearly ready. Tomorrow we shall
   be married!'

THE SECOND COUNCILLOR. She saw there was no hope,

THOUSANDFURS. and the only way out was to run away.

THE THIRD COUNCILLOR. When everyone in the palace was asleep, she gathered together three little things from her treasures:

THOUSANDFURS *holds up these items in turn, as she packs them.*

THE SECOND COUNCILLOR. a gold ring,

THE FIRST COUNCILLOR. a tiny golden spinning wheel

THE THIRD COUNCILLOR. and a little golden bobbin.

THE FIRST COUNCILLOR. She folded the three dresses so small that they fitted into a nutshell,

THE SECOND COUNCILLOR. put on her thousand-fur cloak,

THE THIRD COUNCILLOR. and blackened her face and hands with soot.

THE FIRST COUNCILLOR. Then,

THOUSANDFURS. commending herself to God,

THE SECOND COUNCILLOR. she left the palace

THE THIRD COUNCILLOR. and set out on the high road.

Unseen by THOUSANDFURS, THE KING *follows her, always keeping at a distance.*

THE KING. She walked and walked till she came to a mighty forest.

THE FIRST COUNCILLOR. By that time the night was coming to an end,

THOUSANDFURS. and the first birds were beginning to sing;

THE THIRD COUNCILLOR. and the princess was so tired that she found a hollow tree,

THE SECOND COUNCILLOR. curled up inside it,

THE KING. and was asleep in a moment.

THE FIRST COUNCILLOR. The sun rose, and she was still asleep.

THE THIRD COUNCILLOR. Broad daylight came, and still she slept on.

THE SECOND KING *arrives with* THE THREE HUNTSMEN, *who have three* HOUNDS *straining on leashes*.

THE SECOND KING. Now it happened that the king who owned that forest was out hunting that very morning.

THE KING. His hounds caught the scent of something strange,

THE FIRST HUNTSMAN. and they ran up to the tree and circled it,

THE SECOND HUNTSMAN. barking and barking.

THE SECOND KING. 'There's an animal hiding in there,'

THE THIRD HUNTSMAN. the king said to his huntsmen.

THE SECOND KING. 'Go and see what it is.'

THE KING. They did as he said, and came back to say,

THE FIRST HUNTSMAN. 'It's a strange beast, your majesty,

THE THIRD HUNTSMAN. like nothing we've ever seen in these woods.

THE SECOND HUNTSMAN. Its skin seems to be made of a thousand kinds of fur,

THE FIRST HUNTSMAN. and it's just lying there asleep.'

THE SECOND KING. 'See if you can catch it alive. We'll tie it to the cart and take it back to the castle.'

THE SECOND HUNTSMAN. Taking care

THE THIRD HUNTSMAN. in case she was dangerous,

THE KING. the huntsmen reached into the hollow tree and seized the princess.

THE SECOND KING. She woke up to find herself being dragged out of her hiding place,

THE KING. and full of fear she cried out,

THOUSANDFURS. 'Don't hurt me! I'm a poor girl, that's all! My mother and father abandoned me and I was lost!'

THE FIRST HUNTSMAN. 'Well, Thousandfurs, you're not lost now.'

THE SECOND HUNTSMAN. 'You're a trophy, you are.

THE THIRD HUNTSMAN. You belong to us.

THE FIRST HUNTSMAN. We'll take you to the kitchen

THE SECOND HUNTSMAN. and you can wash the dishes.'

THE SECOND KING. Seeing that she wasn't a rare beast, the king himself lost interest.

THE FIRST HUNTSMAN. The huntsmen set her up on the cart

THE SECOND HUNTSMAN. and off they went,

THOUSANDFURS. bumping over the ruts all the way back to the castle,

THE COOK. where the domestic servants took her in

THE FIRST SERVANT. and showed her a little cubbyhole under the stairs,

THOUSANDFURS. dark and dusty.

THE SECOND SERVANT. 'You can live in there, you furry creature,'

THE THIRD SERVANT. they told her.

THOUSANDFURS. They made her work in the kitchen.

THE THIRD SERVANT. She carried wood and kept the fire going,

THE FIRST SERVANT. she drew water from the well,

THE COOK. she plucked chickens,

THE THIRD SERVANT. she washed and peeled the vegetables,

THE SECOND SERVANT. she washed the greasy dishes –

THE FIRST SERVANT. all the dirty work was given to
Thousandfurs.

THOUSANDFURS. And there she lived as a skivvy for
a long time.

THE KING (*still watching her*). Ah, my lovely princess, what's
to become of you!

THE FIRST BALLGOER. Well, one day it was announced that
the king was to hold a grand ball in the castle.

THE THIRD SERVANT. Thousandfurs was curious to see, and
she said to the cook,

THOUSANDFURS. 'Could I go upstairs and have a look?
I'll stay outside the door.'

THE COOK 'Go on then. But make sure you're back here in
half an hour. Those ashes won't clear themselves.'

The ritual of putting on the ballgown.

THE SECOND SERVANT. Thousandfurs took a lamp and
a bowl of water and went into her cubbyhole.

THE FIRST SERVANT. There she took off her cloak and
washed her hands and face,

THE THIRD SERVANT. so that her beauty was clear to see.

THE SECOND SERVANT. Then she opened the nutshell

THOUSANDFURS. and took out the dress that was as gold
as the sun,

THE FIRST SERVANT. and put that on,

THE THIRD SERVANT. and then she went upstairs to
the ballroom.

Music.

THE FIRST SERVANT. All the servants bowed to her,

THE FIRST BALLGOER. and the guests smiled politely,

THE FOURTH BALLGOER. because everyone thought she
must be a princess.

THE SECOND KING. When the king saw her he felt as if a thunderbolt had struck his heart. He'd never seen such beauty in all his life.

THE SECOND BALLGOER. He danced with her, half-dazed,

THE FIRST BALLGOER. and when the dance was over, she curtseyed

THE SECOND KING. and vanished so quickly that he didn't see where she went.

THE THIRD BALLGOER. He made enquiries of every guard and every sentry:

THE SECOND KING. had she left the castle? Had anyone seen where she'd gone?

THE SECOND BALLGOER. But no one had,

THOUSANDFURS. because she'd slipped away very quickly and gone back to her cubbyhole.

THE THIRD SERVANT. She folded the dress away,

THE FIRST SERVANT. put on her fur cloak,

THE SECOND SERVANT. dirtied her face and hands,

THOUSANDFURS. and once again she was Thousandfurs the kitchen maid.

THE THIRD SERVANT. She began to clear the ashes away, but the cook said,

THE COOK. 'Leave that till tomorrow. I've got another job for you: make some soup for the king while I go and have a look upstairs. But mind you don't let a hair fall into it, or there'll be no food for you from now on.'

THE FIRST SERVANT. The cook went upstairs, and Thousandfurs set about making some bread soup, as well as she knew how.

THOUSANDFURS. When it was ready she got her gold ring and placed it in the king's bowl.

THE FIRST SERVANT. After the ball was over – (*A bell rings in the kitchen.*) the king called for his soup,

THE FIRST SERVANT *hurries to* THE SECOND KING *with the bowl, bows and leaves. The other* SERVANTS *spy on proceedings.*

THE SECOND KING. and it tasted so good that he thought he'd never tasted better.

THE SECOND SERVANT. And when he reached the bottom of the bowl...

THE SECOND KING. 'What's this? A gold ring? How in the world did that get in there? Send for the cook!'

THE COOK. The cook was terrified.

THE THIRD SERVANT. As he hurried out of the kitchen he said to Thousandfurs,

THE COOK. 'You must have let a hair fall in the soup. Didn't I warn you about that? Just you wait till I get back. You'll be black and blue, my girl.'

THE SECOND SERVANT. The cook came before the king,

THE FIRST SERVANT. trembling and twisting his apron in his hands.

THE SECOND KING. 'Did you make this soup? Stop fiddling. Stand up straight.'

THE COOK. 'Yes, your majesty,'

THE SECOND SERVANT. said the cook faintly.

THE SECOND KING. 'You're not telling the truth. This is different from what you normally send up, and it's much better. Who made it, eh?'

THE COOK. 'I'm sorry, your majesty, yes, you're right, sire, it wasn't me; it was that little furry skivvy.'

THE SECOND KING. 'Send her up here.'

THE THIRD SERVANT. When Thousandfurs arrived the king said,

THE SECOND KING. 'Who are you?'

THOUSANDFURS. 'I'm a poor child who has no mother or father.'

THE SECOND KING. 'How did you come to work in my castle?'

THOUSANDFURS. 'I was found in a tree, sire.'

THE SECOND KING. 'Hmm. And where did you get this ring?'

THOUSANDFURS. 'I don't know anything about a ring, your majesty.'

THE SECOND SERVANT. The king thought she must be simple, and dismissed her.

THE SECOND BALLGOER. Some time later there was another ball,

THOUSANDFURS. and as before Thousandfurs asked the cook for permission to go upstairs and have a look.

THE COOK. 'Well, all right. Half an hour, that's all. And then come back here and make that bread soup the king likes so much.'

The dressing ritual again.

THE FIRST SERVANT. Thousandfurs ran to her cubbyhole,

THE THIRD SERVANT. washed herself quickly,

THOUSANDFURS. and put on the dress that was as silver as the moon.

THE FIRST SERVANT. She went up into the ballroom,

Music.

THE SECOND KING. and the king saw her at once through all the crowd of dancers, for she was even more beautiful than before.

THOUSANDFURS. They danced together,

THE SECOND KING. and it only seemed like a moment to him,

THOUSANDFURS. for as soon as the dance was over

THE SECOND KING. she disappeared at once.

THE THIRD SERVANT. She ran down to her cubbyhole, put the dress away,

THOUSANDFURS. and became Thousandfurs again

THE FIRST SERVANT. before hurrying into the kitchen to make some bread soup.

THE SECOND SERVANT. While the cook was upstairs watching the dancing, she put the little golden spinning wheel into the bowl and poured the soup over it.

The bell rings again. This time, THE SECOND SERVANT *serves the food.*

THE FIRST SERVANT. And as before the king found it and sent for the cook,

THE COOK. and the cook admitted that it was again Thousandfurs who'd made it,

THE THIRD SERVANT. so the king sent for her.

THE SECOND KING. 'I have to say I'm puzzled by you. Tell me again where you came from.'

THOUSANDFURS. 'From a hollow tree, your majesty.'

THE SECOND KING. No,

THE FIRST SERVANT. he thought,

THE SECOND KING. the poor girl must have lost her wits. Such a shame – she might be pretty under all that dirt. But she plainly knew nothing about the little golden spinning wheel,

THE SECOND SERVANT. so he sent her away.

THE THIRD BALLGOER. When the king gave a third ball, everything happened as before.

THOUSANDFURS. The cook was getting suspicious, though, and he said,

THE COOK. 'I think you must be a witch, you furry creature. You always put something in the soup that makes the king like it more than mine.'

THE FIRST SERVANT. But he was good-natured enough, and he let her go up and look at the lords and ladies as she'd done before.

The dressing ritual, a third time.

THOUSANDFURS. She put on the dress that glittered like the stars and hurried to the ballroom.

THE SECOND KING. The king had never seen anyone as lovely,

THE FIRST BALLGOER. and he ordered the orchestra to play a very long dance

THE THIRD BALLGOER. so that he might have the chance to talk to her.

Music.

THE SECOND KING. She was as light in his arms as the starlight itself, but she said very little;

THE KING. however, he did manage to slip a ring on her finger without her noticing it.

THOUSANDFURS. When the dance was over her half-hour was up, so she tried to slip away.

THE SECOND BALLGOER. They had a little struggle, because he wanted to hold on to her,

THE SECOND KING. but she was too quick for him and ran out before he could stop her.

THE THIRD SERVANT. When she got back to her cubbyhole, she didn't have time to take the dress off,

THE FIRST SERVANT. so she put her fur cloak on over it and then dirtied herself,

THE SECOND SERVANT. but in her haste she missed one finger, which remained clean.

THE FIRST SERVANT. Then she hurried to make the soup,

THOUSANDFURS. and while the cook was upstairs she put her golden bobbin into it just as before.

The bell rings, a third time. THE THIRD SERVANT *presents the bowl of soup.*

THE THIRD SERVANT. When the king found the bobbin he didn't waste time calling the cook, but sent for Thousandfurs directly.

THE SECOND SERVANT. As soon as she came,

THE SECOND KING. he saw her one white finger, and the ring he'd put on it while they were dancing.

THE THIRD SERVANT. He seized her hand and held it fast,

THE FIRST SERVANT. and as she struggled

THOUSANDFURS. the fur cloak came open a little

THE SECOND KING. and revealed the glitter of the starry dress.

THE THIRD SERVANT. The king pushed back the hood of her cloak,

THE SECOND SERVANT. and her gold hair fell down;

THOUSANDFURS. and then he pulled the cloak off altogether,

THE SECOND KING. and revealed the lovely princess he'd been dancing with not half an hour before.

THE FIRST SERVANT. When her face and hands were washed, no one could deny that she was more beautiful than anyone who had ever lived.

THE SECOND KING. 'You shall be my dearest bride. And we shall never part.'

THE THIRD SERVANT. Their wedding was celebrated soon afterwards,

THE SECOND KING. and they lived happily

THOUSANDFURS. for the rest of their lives.

Suddenly, among the courtiers, THOUSANDFURS *sees –
her father! She gasps and points him out. The* HOUNDS *are
released, and chase* THE KING *from the palace.*

The Goose Girl at the Spring

There are three main locations in this Tale: the humble abode of
THE OLD WOMAN *and* THE GOOSE GIRL, *the royal palace
– and the deep forest, with its spring. In this story,* THE
GOOSE GIRL *often observes* THE YOUNG COUNT. *In the
original production, she wore something akin to a beekeeper's
hat as a veil: this she removed during the ritual of the washing
of the skin. There was a gaggle of geese puppets.*

*This Tale is unusual, insofar as it has a tale-within-a-tale. And
is incomplete…*

THE QUEEN. Once upon a time

THE OLD WOMAN. there was a very old woman

THE YOUNG COUNT. who lived with her flock of geese

THE GOOSE GIRL. in a lonely place among the mountains,

THE KING. where her little house lay surrounded by a
   deep forest.

THE GOOSE GIRL. Every morning she took her crutch and
   hobbled off into the woods, where she kept herself busy

THE KING. gathering grass for her geese and picking any wild
   fruit she could reach.

THE YOUNG COUNT. She put it all on her back and carried
   it home.

THE QUEEN. If she met anyone on the path, she would always
   greet them in a friendly way, saying,

THE OLD WOMAN. 'Good day, neighbour! Nice weather!
   Yes, it's grass I've got here, as much as I can carry; we poor
   people all have to bear our burdens.'

THE GOOSE GIRL. But for some reason people didn't like
   meeting her.

THE YOUNG COUNT. When they saw her coming, they'd often take a different path,

A LITTLE BOY *watches*.

THE OLD WOMAN. and if a father and his little boy came across her, the father would whisper,

A FATHER. 'Beware of that old woman. She's a crafty one. It wouldn't surprise me if she was a witch.'

And he drags his inquisitive son away.

THE GOOSE GIRL. One morning a good-looking young man happened to be walking through the forest.

THE YOUNG COUNT. The sun was shining, the birds were singing, a fresh breeze stirred the leaves, and he was feeling happy and cheerful.

THE QUEEN. He hadn't seen anyone else that morning,

THE KING. but suddenly he came across the old witch kneeling on the ground cutting grass with a sickle.

THE GOOSE GIRL. There was already a big load of grass neatly cut, and beside it two baskets filled with wild apples and pears.

THE YOUNG COUNT. 'Good grief, my dear old woman – you can't be intending to carry all that!'

THE OLD WOMAN. 'Oh, yes, I must, sir. Rich people don't have to do that sort of thing, but we poor folk have a saying: "Don't look back, you'll only see how bent you are." Would you be able to help me, I wonder, sir? You've got a fine straight back and a strong pair of legs. I'm sure you could manage it easily. It's not far to go, my little house, just out of sight over that way.'

THE QUEEN. The young man felt sorry for her, and said,

THE YOUNG COUNT. 'Well, I'm one of those rich people, I have to confess – my father's a nobleman – but I'm happy to show you that farmers aren't the only people who can carry things. Yes, I'll take the bundle to your house for you.'

THE OLD WOMAN. 'That's very good of you, sir. It might take an hour's walking, but I'm sure you won't mind that. You could carry the apples and pears for me too.'

THE QUEEN. The young count began to have second thoughts when she mentioned an hour's walk,

THE YOUNG COUNT. but she was so quick to take up his offer that he couldn't back out of it.

THE KING. She wrapped the grass up in a cloth and tied it on to his back

THE GOOSE GIRL. and then put the baskets into his hands.

THE OLD WOMAN. 'You see: not much really.'

She lets go of the handles: THE YOUNG COUNT *discovers that the baskets weigh a tonne.*

THE YOUNG COUNT. 'But it's actually quite heavy. This grass – is it grass? It feels like bricks! And the fruit might as well be blocks of stone. I can hardly breathe!'

THE KING. He would have liked to put it all down, but he didn't want to face the old woman's mockery.

THE QUEEN. She was already teasing him cruelly.

THE OLD WOMAN. 'Look at the fine young gentleman, making such a fuss about what a poor old woman has to carry every day! You're good with words, aren't you? "Farmers aren't the only people who can carry things!" But when it comes to deeds, you fall at the first hurdle. Come on! What are you standing around for? Get a move on! Nobody's going to do it for you.'

THE YOUNG COUNT. While he walked on level ground he could just about bear the weight,

THE QUEEN. but as soon as the path began to slope upwards

THE KING. his feet rolled on the stones,

THE QUEEN. which slipped out as if they were alive,

THE KING. and he could barely move.

THE GOOSE GIRL. Beads of sweat appeared on his face and trickled hot and cold down his back.

THE YOUNG COUNT. 'I can't go any further… I've got to stop and rest.'

THE OLD WOMAN. 'Oh, no, you don't. You can stop and rest when we've got there, but till then you keep walking. You never know – it might bring you luck.'

THE YOUNG COUNT. 'Oh, this is too much. This is outrageous!'

THE KING. He tried to throw off the bundle, but he just couldn't dislodge it.

THE YOUNG COUNT. It clung to his back as if it were growing there.

THE GOOSE GIRL. He squirmed and twisted this way and that,

THE QUEEN. and the old woman laughed at him and jumped up and down with her crutch.

THE OLD WOMAN. 'No point in losing your temper, young sir. You're as red in the face as a turkey cock. Carry your burden patiently, and when we get home, I might give you a tip.'

THE KING. What could he do?

THE QUEEN. He had to stumble on after the old woman as well as he could.

THE KING. The odd thing was that while his load seemed to be getting heavier and heavier,

THE QUEEN. she seemed to be getting more and more nimble.

THE GOOSE GIRL. Then all of a sudden she gave a skip and landed right on top of the pack on his back

THE KING. and stayed there.

THE QUEEN. She was as thin as a stick,

THE YOUNG COUNT. but she weighed more than the stoutest peasant girl.

THE OLD WOMAN. The young man's legs wobbled,

THE YOUNG COUNT. all his muscles trembled with effort and blazed with pain,

THE KING. and whenever he tried to stop for a moment, the old woman lashed him with a bunch of stinging nettles.

THE GOOSE GIRL. He groaned,

THE OLD WOMAN. he sobbed,

THE YOUNG COUNT. he struggled on,

THE QUEEN. and when he was sure he was going to collapse,

THE YOUNG COUNT. they turned a corner in the path

THE OLD WOMAN. and there was the old woman's house.

Two STORYTELLERS *arrive with the geese puppets.*

THE KING. When the geese saw her,

THE QUEEN. they stretched out their necks and their wings

THE KING. and ran towards her, cackling.

THE YOUNG COUNT. After them came another old woman, carrying a stick.

THE QUEEN. This one wasn't as old as the first one,

THE KING. but she was big and strong with a heavy, dull, ugly face.

THE GOOSE GIRL. 'Where've you been, Mother? You've been gone so long I thought something must have happened to you.'

THE OLD WOMAN. 'Oh, no, my pretty one. I met this kind gentleman and he offered to carry my bundle for me. And look, he even offered to take me on his back when I got tired. We had such a nice conversation that the journey passed in no time.'

THE QUEEN. Finally the old woman slid off the young count's back and took the bundle and the baskets.

THE OLD WOMAN. 'There we are, sir – you sit yourself down and have a breather. You've earned your little reward, and you shall have it. (*To* THE GOOSE GIRL.) As for you, my beautiful treasure, you better go inside. It wouldn't be proper for you to stay alone with a lusty young fellow like this. I know what young men are like. He might fall in love with you.'

THE KING. The count didn't know whether to laugh or to cry;

THE YOUNG COUNT. even if she were thirty years younger, he thought, this treasure would never prompt a flicker in his heart.

THE QUEEN. The old woman fussed over her geese as if they were children before going inside after her daughter.

THE GOOSE GIRL. The young man stretched himself out on a bench under an apple tree.

THE YOUNG COUNT. It was a beautiful morning; the sun shone warmly, the air was mild, and all around him stretched a green meadow covered with cowslips and wild thyme and a thousand other flowers.

THE KING. A clear stream twinkled in the sunlight as it ran through the middle of the meadow,

THE GOOSE GIRL. and the white geese waddled here and there or paddled in the stream.

THE YOUNG COUNT. 'What a lovely place. But I'm so tired I can't keep my eyes open. I think I'll take a nap for a few minutes. I just hope the wind doesn't blow my legs away; they're as weak as tinder.'

And he dozes off...

THE QUEEN. The next thing he knew, the old woman was shaking his arm.

THE OLD WOMAN. 'Wakey wakey, you can't stay here. I admit I gave you a hard time, but you're still alive, and here's your reward. I said I'd give you something, didn't I? You don't need money or land, so here's something else. Look after it well and it'll bring you luck.'

THE YOUNG COUNT. What she gave him was a little box carved out of a single emerald.

THE KING. The count jumped up, feeling refreshed by his sleep,

THE QUEEN. and thanked her for the gift.

THE GOOSE GIRL. Then he set out on his way without once looking back for the beautiful treasure.

THE KING. For a long way down the path he could still hear the happy noise of the geese.

THE OLD WOMAN. He wandered in the forest for at least three days before he found his way out.

THE YOUNG COUNT. Eventually he came to a large city,

THE GOOSE GIRL. where the custom was that every stranger had to be brought before the king and queen;

THE YOUNG COUNT. so he was taken to the palace, where the king and queen were sitting on their thrones.

THE OLD WOMAN. The young count knelt politely, and since he had nothing else to offer, he took the emerald box from his pocket, opened it and set it down before the queen.

THE GOOSE GIRL. She beckoned to him to bring the box closer so that she could look inside it,

THE YOUNG COUNT. but no sooner had she seen what was there than she fell into a dead faint.

THE FIRST BODYGUARD. The bodyguards seized the young man at once

THE SECOND BODYGUARD. and were about to drag him off to prison

THE KING. when the queen opened her eyes.

THE QUEEN. 'Release him! Everyone must leave the throne room. I want to speak to this young man in private.'

THE YOUNG COUNT. When they were alone, the queen began to cry bitterly.

Here, we enter into a tale-within-a-tale. The fact that this is related by one storyteller, rather than shared, is deliberate, and its oddity should be celebrated. Besides, if it were to be acted out, the identity of THE GOOSE GIRL *would be revealed, ruining the surprise.*

THE QUEEN. 'What use is all the splendour of this palace?
Every morning when I wake up, sorrow rushes in on me like
a flood. I once had three daughters, and the third was so
beautiful that everyone thought she was a miracle. She was
as white as snow and as pink as apple blossoms, and her
hair shone like the beams of the sun. When she wept, it
wasn't tears that flowed down her cheeks but pearls and
precious stones.

On her fifteenth birthday, the king called all three daughters to
his throne. You can't imagine how everyone blinked when the
third daughter came in – it was just as if the sun had come out.

The king said, "My daughters, since I don't know when my
last day will arrive, I'm going to decide today what each of
you shall receive after my death. You all love me, but whoever
loves me most shall have the largest part of the kingdom."

Each of the girls said she loved him most of all, but he
wanted more than that.

"Tell me exactly how much you love me," he said. "Then I'll
know just what you mean."

The oldest daughter said, "I love you as much as the sweetest
sugar." The second daughter said, "I love you as much as I
love my prettiest dress."

But the third daughter didn't say a word. So her father said,
"And you, darling, how much do you love me?"

And she said, "I don't know. I can't compare my love
with anything."

But he kept on and on demanding an answer until she found
something to compare her love to, and she said, "No matter
how good the food, it won't taste of anything without salt.
So I love my father as much as I love salt."

When the king heard this, he became furious and said,

"If that's how you love me, then that's how your love will
be rewarded."

And he divided his kingdom between the two eldest
daughters, and he ordered the youngest to have a sack of salt
bound to her back, and then two servants were to lead her

out into the depths of the forest. We all begged and pleaded for mercy, but he wouldn't change his mind. Oh, how she wept when she was forced to leave! The path she'd trodden was covered with pearls.

Not long afterwards, the king regretted what he'd done, and had the forest searched from end to end; but she was never found.

When I think that wild animals may have eaten her, I can hardly bear the pain. Sometimes I comfort myself by thinking that she's found shelter in a cave, or she's being looked after by kind people, but...

So you can imagine the shock when I opened the emerald box and saw a pearl just like the ones my daughter wept. And you can imagine how my heart was stirred. And now you must tell me: where did you get this? How does it come to be in your possession?'

THE YOUNG COUNT. The young count told her how it had been given to him by the old woman in the forest, who he believed must be a witch, because everything about her had made him feel uneasy.

THE QUEEN. However, he said, this was the first he had heard about the queen's daughter.

THE KING. Accordingly, the king and queen decided to set out at once to find the old woman,

THE QUEEN. in the hope that she might be able to give them some news about their child.

THE KING. That evening the old woman was sitting in her little house, spinning with her spinning wheel.

THE OLD WOMAN. Night was falling, and the only light came from a pine log burning on the hearth.

THE QUEEN. Suddenly there were loud cries from outside, as the geese came home from their pasture,

THE KING. and a moment later the daughter entered the house,

THE GOOSE GIRL. but the old woman merely nodded and didn't say a word.

THE YOUNG COUNT. Her daughter sat down beside her and took up her own spinning, twisting the thread as deftly as any young girl.

THE QUEEN. The two of them sat together for two hours without exchanging a word.

THE KING. Finally there came a rustling from the window,

THE GOOSE GIRL. and they looked up to see two fiery red eyes glaring in at them.

THE YOUNG COUNT. It was an old owl, who cried out,

THE OWL. 'Tu-whoo, tu-whoo,'

THE YOUNG COUNT. three times.

THE OWL. 'Tu-whoo.'

THE QUEEN. The old woman said,

THE OLD WOMAN. 'Well, my little daughter, it's time for you to go outside and do your work.'

THE KING. The daughter stood up.

THE YOUNG COUNT. Where did she go?

THE QUEEN. Out across the meadow, and down towards the valley,

THE KING. until she came to three old oak trees next to a spring.

THE GOOSE GIRL. The moon was full, and had just risen over the mountain;

THE QUEEN. it was so bright that you could have found a pin on the ground.

And we witness a strange ritual.

THE OLD WOMAN. The daughter unfastened the skin at her neck, and pulled her face right over her head before kneeling down at the spring and washing herself.

THE KING. When she'd done that, she dipped the skin of her false face in the water, wrung it out, and laid it to dry and bleach on the grass.

THE QUEEN. But what a change had come over her! You wouldn't believe it!

THE KING. After the dull heavy face and the grey wig had come off, her hair flowed down like liquid sunlight.

THE QUEEN. Her eyes sparkled like stars, and her cheeks were as pink as the freshest apple blossom.

THE OLD WOMAN. But this girl, so beautiful, was sad.

THE KING. She sat down by the spring and cried bitterly.

THE QUEEN. Tear after tear rolled down her long hair and fell into the grass.

THE OLD WOMAN. There she sat, and she would have stayed there for a long time if she hadn't heard

THE GOOSE GIRL. a rustling among the branches of a tree nearby.

THE KING. Like a deer startled by the sound of a hunter's rifle, she jumped up at once.

THE QUEEN. At the same time a dark cloud passed over the face of the moon, and in the sudden darkness the maiden slipped into the old skin and vanished like a candle flame blown out by the wind.

THE KING. Shivering like an aspen leaf, she ran back to the little house, where the old woman was standing by the door.

THE GOOSE GIRL. 'Oh, Mother, I – '

THE OLD WOMAN. 'Hush, dear. I know, I know.'

THE QUEEN. She led the girl into the room and put another log on the fire.

THE KING. But she didn't go back to the spinning wheel; she took a broom and began to sweep the floor.

THE OLD WOMAN. 'We must make everything neat and clean.'

THE GOOSE GIRL. 'But, Mother, what are you doing it now for? It's late! What's happening?'

THE OLD WOMAN. 'Don't you know what time it is?'

THE GOOSE GIRL. 'It's not past midnight, but it must be past eleven.'

THE OLD WOMAN. 'And don't you remember that it was three years ago today when you came to me? Time's up, my dear. We can't stay together any longer.'

THE KING. The girl was frightened.

THE GOOSE GIRL. 'Oh, Mother dear, you're not really going to throw me out, are you? Where shall I go? I've got no friends, I've got no home to go to. I've done everything you've asked of me, you've always been satisfied with my work – please don't send me away!'

THE QUEEN. But the old woman wouldn't give her an answer.

THE OLD WOMAN. 'My own time here is up. But before I leave, the house must be spick and span. So don't get in my way, and don't worry too much either. You'll find a roof to shelter you, and you'll be quite satisfied with the wages I'm going to give you.'

THE GOOSE GIRL. 'But please tell me, what's happening?'

THE OLD WOMAN. 'I've told you once, and I'm telling you again: don't interrupt my work. Go to your room, take the skin off your face, and put on the silk dress you were wearing when you first came here. Then wait there till I call you.'

THE GOOSE GIRL *goes to her room – then the tale jump-cuts to the other group, earlier in the story.*

THE KING. Meanwhile, the king and queen were continuing their search for the old woman who had given the count the emerald box.

THE QUEEN. He had gone with them,

THE YOUNG COUNT. but he'd become separated from them in the thick forest, and he'd had to go on alone.

THE OLD WOMAN. He thought he'd found the right path, but then as the daylight waned he thought he'd better not go any further in case he got really lost;

THE KING. so he climbed a tree, meaning to spend the night safely up among the branches.

THE QUEEN. But when the moon came out he saw something moving down the meadow, and in its brilliant light he realised

THE YOUNG COUNT. it was the goose girl he'd seen before at the old woman's house.

THE KING. She was coming towards the trees, and he thought,

THE YOUNG COUNT. 'Aha! If I catch one of these witches, I'll soon have my hands on the other.'

And we see the washing ritual from before, although now from another perspective.

THE QUEEN. But then she stopped at the spring,

THE GOOSE GIRL. and removed her skin,

THE OLD WOMAN. and the count nearly fell out of the tree with astonishment;

THE YOUNG COUNT. and when her golden hair fell down around her shoulders, and he saw her clearly in the moonlight, he knew that she was more beautiful than anyone he had ever seen.

THE KING. He hardly dared to breathe.

THE QUEEN. But he couldn't resist leaning forward to get a little closer, and in doing so he leaned too heavily on a dry branch – (*Crack!*)

THE KING. and it was the sound of it cracking that startled her.

THE QUEEN. She leaped up at once and put on the other skin,

THE OLD WOMAN. and then the cloud passed in front of the moon;

THE GOOSE GIRL. and in the sudden darkness she slipped away.

THE YOUNG COUNT. The count climbed down from the tree at once and ran after her.

THE OLD WOMAN. He hadn't gone very far up the meadow when he saw two figures making for the house.

THE YOUNG COUNT. It was the king and queen,

THE QUEEN. who'd seen the firelight in the window,

THE KING. and when the count caught up with them and told them about the miracle he'd seen at the spring,

THE QUEEN. they were sure the girl must be their daughter.

THE YOUNG COUNT. Full of joy and hope, they hurried on and soon arrived at the little house.

THE KING. The geese were all asleep with their heads tucked under their wings, and not one of them moved.

THE QUEEN. The three searchers looked in at the window,

THE KING. and saw the old woman quietly sitting and spinning, nodding her head as she turned the wheel.

THE QUEEN. Everything in the room was as clean as if the little fog men lived there, who carry no dust on their feet;

THE YOUNG COUNT. but there was no sign of the princess.

THE KING. For a minute or two the king and queen just looked in,

THE QUEEN. but then they plucked up their courage and knocked at the window.

THE KING. The old woman seemed to be expecting them.

THE YOUNG COUNT. She stood up and called out in a friendly voice,

THE OLD WOMAN. 'Come in. I know who you are.'

THE QUEEN. When they were all inside the house, the old woman said,

THE OLD WOMAN. 'You could have spared yourself this sorrow and this journey, you know, if you hadn't banished your daughter so unjustly three years ago. But she hasn't come to harm. She's tended the geese for three years, and made a good job of it. She's learned nothing evil and she's kept a pure heart. But I think you've been punished enough by the unhappiness you've suffered.'

THE YOUNG COUNT. Then she went to the door and said,

THE OLD WOMAN. 'Come out, my little daughter.'

THE KING. The door opened,

THE QUEEN. and the princess came into the room, wearing her silken dress, with her golden hair shining and her bright eyes sparkling.

THE GOOSE GIRL *has been transformed.*

THE YOUNG COUNT. It was as if an angel had come down from heaven.

THE OLD WOMAN. The princess went straight to her mother and father and embraced them both, and kissed them.

THE QUEEN. Both of them wept for joy;

THE KING. they couldn't help it.

THE OLD WOMAN. The young count was standing nearby,

THE YOUNG COUNT. and when she caught sight of him her cheeks became as red as a moss rose,

THE PRINCESS. and she herself didn't know why.

THE QUEEN. The king said,

THE KING. 'My dear child, I gave my kingdom away. What can I give you?'

THE OLD WOMAN. 'She needs nothing. I shall give her the tears she shed because of you. Each one is a pearl more precious than any they find in the sea, and they're worth more than your whole kingdom. And as a reward for looking after the geese, I shall give her my house.'

A vibration, as if in an earthquake.

THE KING. And just as the old woman said that, she vanished.

THE QUEEN. The walls of the house rumbled and shook,

THE YOUNG COUNT. and when the king and queen and the princess and the count looked around,

THE PRINCESS. they saw that it had been changed into a beautiful palace.

THE YOUNG COUNT. A table had been set with a feast fit for an emperor,

THE PRINCESS. and there were servants bustling everywhere to do their bidding.

THE OLD WOMAN*'s house has been transformed, but then… a moment of awkwardness. Has something gone wrong? The* STORYTELLERS *turn and address the audience directly, as themselves.*

THE KING. The story doesn't end there.

THE YOUNG COUNT. The trouble is that my grandmother, who told it to me, is losing her memory, and she's forgotten the rest. But I think that the beautiful princess married the count, and they remained together and lived in happiness.

THE GOOSE GIRL. As for the snow-white geese, some say that they were really girls that the old woman had taken into her care, and it's likely that they regained their human form and stayed there to serve the young queen.

THE OLD WOMAN. I wouldn't be surprised.

THE QUEEN. As for the old woman, she can't have been a witch, as people thought, but a wise woman who meant well.

THE YOUNG COUNT. Why did she treat the young count like that when he first came across her?

THE KING. Well, who knows? She might have seen into his character and found a seed or two of arrogance there.

THE YOUNG COUNT. If so, she knew how to deal with it.

THE QUEEN. Finally, it's almost certain that she was present at the birth of the princess,

THE KING. and gave her the gift of weeping pearls instead of tears.

THE GOOSE GIRL. That doesn't happen much any more.

THE OLD WOMAN. If it did, poor people would soon become rich.

Hansel and Gretel

THE WOODCUTTER *and his family live in a very simple home, beside a dark and threatening forest. Other key locations are* THE WITCH*'s house, both outside and inside, with a kitchen that has the feel of an abattoir; and a shed, like a torture cell. Darkness and light – often moonlight – is important.*

There are two 'bad angels' in this Tale, THE WITCH *and* THE STEPMOTHER. *Sometimes in the storytelling they vie for power, but share a glee in the misfortune which befalls the children.* THE WOODCUTTER *and* THE WHITE DUCK, *meanwhile, are the forces for good.*

THE WOODCUTTER. At the edge of a great forest lived a poor woodcutter

THE STEPMOTHER. with his wife

THE WITCH. and his two children,

HANSEL. a boy called Hansel

GRETEL. and a girl called Gretel.

A family portrait.

THE WOODCUTTER. The family had little to eat at the best of times,

HANSEL. and what's more there was a famine in the land,

GRETEL. and often the father couldn't even provide their daily bread.

THE WITCH. One night

THE WOODCUTTER. as he lay in bed worrying about their poverty,

THE WITCH. he sighed and said to his wife,

THE WOODCUTTER. 'What's going to become of us? How can we keep the children fed when we haven't any food for ourselves?'

THE STEPMOTHER. 'I tell you what. This is what we'll do. Early tomorrow morning we'll take them into the thickest part of the forest, make them comfortable, light a fire to keep them warm, give them a little bit of bread, and then leave them there by themselves. They won't find their way home, and we'll be rid of them.'

THE WOODCUTTER. 'No, no, no. I won't do that. Abandon my own children in the forest? Never! Wild animals would tear them to pieces.'

THE STEPMOTHER. 'You're a fool. If we don't get rid of them, all four of us will starve. You may as well start planing the wood for our coffins.'

THE WITCH. She gave him no peace until he gave in.

THE WOODCUTTER. 'But I don't like it. I can't help feeling sorry for them...'

GRETEL. In the next room, the children were awake.

HANSEL. They couldn't sleep because they were so hungry,

GRETEL. And they heard every word their stepmother said.

HANSEL. Gretel wept bitterly and whispered,

GRETEL. 'Oh, Hansel, it's the end for us!'

HANSEL. 'Hush. Stop worrying. I know what we can do.'

THE WITCH. As soon as the grown-ups had fallen asleep,

GRETEL. Hansel got out of bed,

HANSEL. put on his old jacket,

GRETEL. opened the lower half of the door

HANSEL. and crept outside.

THE WITCH. The moon was shining brightly,

HANSEL. and the white pebbles in front of the house glittered like silver coins.

GRETEL. Hansel crouched down and filled his pockets with as many as he could cram in.

THE WITCH. Then he went back inside and got into bed and whispered,

HANSEL. 'Don't worry, Gretel. Go to sleep now. God will look after us. Anyway, I've got a plan.'

THE WITCH. At daybreak, even before the sun had risen, the woman came in and pulled the covers off their bed.

THE STEPMOTHER. 'Get up, you layabouts! We're going into the forest to get some wood.'

GRETEL. She gave them each a slice of dry bread.

THE STEPMOTHER. 'That's your lunch – and don't gobble it up too soon, because there's nothing else.'

HANSEL. Gretel put the bread in her apron,

GRETEL. because Hansel's pockets were full of pebbles.

THE WOODCUTTER. They all set off together into the forest.

THE STEPMOTHER. From time to time Hansel would stop and look back at the house, until finally his father said,

THE WOODCUTTER. 'What are you doing, boy? Keep up. Use your legs.'

HANSEL. 'I'm looking at my white kitten. He's sitting on the roof. He wants to say goodbye to me.'

THE STEPMOTHER. 'Stupid boy. That's not your kitten, it's the sun shining on the chimney.'

GRETEL. In fact, Hansel had been dropping the pebbles one by one on the path behind them.

HANSEL. He was looking back because he wanted to make sure they could be seen.

THE WITCH. When they got to the middle of the forest their father said,

THE WOODCUTTER. 'Go and fetch some kindling. I'll make a fire so you won't freeze.'

THE STEPMOTHER. The children gathered some small twigs,

GRETEL. a whole pile of them,

HANSEL. and their father set them alight.

THE WOODCUTTER. When the fire was burning well the woman said,

THE STEPMOTHER. 'Make yourselves comfortable, my dears. Lie down by the fire and snuggle up warm. We'll go off and cut some wood now, and when we've finished we'll come and get you.'

THE WOODCUTTER. Hansel and Gretel sat down by the fire.

THE WITCH. When they felt it must be midday they ate their bread.

An ominous chopping sound.

HANSEL. They could hear the sound of an axe not far away,

GRETEL. so they thought their father was nearby;

THE STEPMOTHER. but it wasn't an axe, it was a branch that he'd tied to a dead tree.

THE WOODCUTTER. The wind swung it back and forth, so it knocked on the wood.

THE WITCH. The children sat there for a long time,

THE STEPMOTHER. and gradually their eyelids began to feel heavy.

THE WITCH. As the afternoon went past and the light faded,

THE STEPMOTHER. they leaned closer together

THE WITCH. and fell sound asleep.

THE WOODCUTTER. They awoke to find themselves in darkness.

HANSEL. Gretel began to cry.

GRETEL. 'How can we ever find our way out?'

HANSEL. 'Wait till the moon comes up. Then you'll see how my plan will work.'

THE WITCH. When the moon did come up it was full and brilliant,

GRETEL. and the white stones Hansel had dropped shone like newly minted coins.

THE WITCH. Hand in hand, the two children followed the trail all through the night,

HANSEL. and just as dawn was breaking, they arrived at their father's house.

GRETEL. The door was locked,

THE WITCH. so they knocked loudly. (*Knock knock knock.*) When the woman opened it her eyes opened too, in shock.

THE STEPMOTHER. 'You wretched children! You made us so worried!'

HANSEL. And she hugged them so tightly

GRETEL. they couldn't breathe.

THE STEPMOTHER. 'Why did you sleep so long? We thought you didn't want to come back!'

GRETEL. And she pinched their cheeks

HANSEL. as if she were really glad to see them.

THE WITCH. When their father came down a moment later, the relief and joy in his face was real,

THE WOODCUTTER. because he hadn't wanted to leave them at all.

THE STEPMOTHER. So that time they were safe.

THE WOODCUTTER. But not long afterwards, food was short again, and many people went hungry.

THE WITCH. One night the children heard the woman say to their father,

THE STEPMOTHER. 'It's no good. We've only got half a loaf left, and then we'll all starve. We must get rid of the children, and do it properly this time. They must have had some trick before, but if we take them deep enough into the woods they'll never find their way out.'

THE WOODCUTTER. 'Oh, I don't like it. There's not just wild animals in the forest, you know. There are goblins and

witches and the Lord knows what. Wouldn't it be better to
share the loaf with the children?'

THE STEPMOTHER. 'Don't be stupid. Where's the sense in
that? You're soft, that's the trouble with you. Soft and stupid.'

THE WITCH. She tore him to shreds with her criticism,

THE STEPMOTHER. and he had no defence;

THE WOODCUTTER. if you've given in once, you have to
give in ever after.

HANSEL. The children were awake,

GRETEL. and they had heard the conversation.

THE WITCH. When the adults were asleep, Hansel got up and
tried to go outside again,

THE STEPMOTHER. but the woman had locked the door and
hidden the key.

THE WITCH. Nevertheless, he comforted his sister when he
got back into bed, and said,

HANSEL. 'Don't worry, Gretel. Go to sleep now. God will
protect us.'

THE STEPMOTHER. Early next morning the woman came and
woke the children as she'd done before,

HANSEL. and gave them each a piece of bread,

GRETEL. though it was even smaller this time.

THE WOODCUTTER. As they went into the forest,

GRETEL. Hansel crumbled his bread up and dropped the
crumbs on the path,

HANSEL. stopping every so often to make sure he could
see them.

THE WOODCUTTER. 'Hansel, keep going. Stop looking back
all the time.'

HANSEL. 'I was looking at my pigeon sitting on the roof. She
wants to say goodbye to me.'

THE STEPMOTHER. 'That's not your pigeon, you fool, it's the sun shining on the chimney. Stop dawdling.'

THE WITCH. Hansel didn't look back again, but he kept crumbling up the bread in his pocket and dropping it on the path.

HANSEL. The woman made them all walk fast,

GRETEL. and they went deeper into the forest than they'd ever gone in all their lives.

THE WITCH. Finally she said,

THE STEPMOTHER. 'This'll do,'

THE WOODCUTTER. and once again they made a fire for the children to sit by.

THE STEPMOTHER. 'Now don't you move. Sit here and don't budge till we come and get you. We've got enough to worry about without you wandering off. We'll be back in the evening.'

THE WITCH. The children sat there until they felt it must be midday,

THE WOODCUTTER. and then they shared Gretel's little piece of bread,

GRETEL. because Hansel had used all his up.

THE STEPMOTHER. Then they fell asleep,

THE WOODCUTTER. and the whole day went by,

THE STEPMOTHER. but no one came for them.

GRETEL. It was dark when they woke up.

HANSEL. 'Hush, don't cry. When the moon comes up, we'll see the crumbs and find our way home.'

THE WITCH. The moon came up,

GRETEL. and they began to look for the crumbs,

HANSEL. but they couldn't find any.

GRETEL. The thousands of birds that fly about in the woods and the fields had pecked them all up.

HANSEL. 'We'll find our way.'

THE STEPMOTHER. But no matter which way they went, they couldn't find the way home.

HANSEL. They walked all through the night

GRETEL. and then all through the following day,

HANSEL. and still they were lost.

GRETEL. They were hungry, too,

HANSEL. terribly hungry,

THE WOODCUTTER. because all they'd had to eat was a few berries that they'd found.

THE STEPMOTHER. They were so tired by this time that they lay down under a tree

THE WITCH. and fell asleep at once.

THE WOODCUTTER. And when they awoke on the third morning,

THE STEPMOTHER. and struggled to their feet,

HANSEL. they were still lost,

GRETEL. and with every step they seemed to be going deeper and deeper into the forest.

HANSEL. If they didn't find help soon, they'd die.

THE SNOW-WHITE BIRD *appears*.

THE WOODCUTTER. But at midday, they saw a little snow-white bird sitting on a branch nearby.

GRETEL. It sang so beautifully that they stopped to listen,

HANSEL. and when it stretched its wings and flew a little way ahead,

GRETEL. they followed it.

THE WOODCUTTER. It perched and sang again,

GRETEL. and again flew a little way ahead,

HANSEL. moving no faster than they could walk,

GRETEL. so that it really seemed to be guiding them.

THE STEPMOTHER. And all of a sudden they found themselves in front of a little house.

The famous house in the woods – not gingerbread, in this version.

GRETEL. The bird perched on the roof,

HANSEL. and there was something strange about the look of that roof.

THE STEPMOTHER. In fact –

HANSEL. 'It's made of cake!'

THE WOODCUTTER. And as for the walls—

GRETEL. 'They're made of bread!'

THE STEPMOTHER. And as for the windows,

HANSEL *and* GRETEL. they were made of sugar.

THE WOODCUTTER. The poor children were so hungry that they didn't even think of knocking at the door and asking permission.

GRETEL. Hansel broke off a piece of roof,

HANSEL. and Gretel knocked through a window,

THE WOODCUTTER. and they sat down right where they were and started to eat at once.

THE STEPMOTHER. After a good few mouthfuls, they heard a soft voice from inside:

THE OLD WOMAN.
'Nibble, nibble, little mouse,
Who's that nibbling at my house?'

THE WOODCUTTER. The children answered:

HANSEL.
'The wind so wild,

GRETEL.
The Heavenly Child.'

THE STEPMOTHER. And then they went on eating,

HANSEL. they were so ravenous.

THE WOODCUTTER. Hansel liked the taste of the roof so much that he pulled off a piece as long as his arm,

THE STEPMOTHER. and Gretel carefully pushed out another windowpane and started crunching her way through it.

HANSEL. Suddenly the door opened

GRETEL. and an old, old woman came hobbling out.

THE WOODCUTTER. Hansel and Gretel were so surprised that they stopped eating and stared at her with their mouths full.

THE STEPMOTHER. But the old woman shook her head and said,

THE OLD WOMAN. 'Don't be frightened, my little dears! Who brought you here? Just come inside, my darlings, come and rest your poor selves in my little box of treats. It's as safe as houses!'

THE WOODCUTTER. She pinched their cheeks fondly,

THE STEPMOTHER. and took each of them by the hand

THE OLD WOMAN. and led them into the cottage.

GRETEL. As if she'd known they were coming,

HANSEL. there was a table laid with two places,

GRETEL. and she served them a delicious meal of milk

HANSEL. and pancakes with sugar and spices,

GRETEL. and apples

HANSEL. and nuts.

THE STEPMOTHER. After that she showed them into a little bedroom where two beds were made up ready, with snow-white sheets.

GRETEL. Hansel and Gretel went to bed,

HANSEL. thinking they were in heaven,

THE WOODCUTTER. and fell asleep at once.

THE OLD WOMAN *drops the pretence and reveals herself to be* THE WITCH.

THE WITCH. But the old woman had only pretended to be friendly.

THE STEPMOTHER. In fact she was a wicked witch, and she had built her delicious house in order to lure children to her.

THE WOODCUTTER. Once she'd captured a child, whether a boy or a girl,

THE WITCH. she killed them, cooked them, and ate them.

THE STEPMOTHER. It was a feast day for her when that happened.

THE WOODCUTTER. Like other witches, she had red eyes and couldn't see very far,

THE WITCH. but she had a keen sense of smell, and she knew at once when humans were nearby.

THE STEPMOTHER. Once Hansel and Gretel were tucked up in bed, she laughed and rubbed her knobbly hands together.

THE WITCH. 'I've got 'em now! They won't get away from me!'

THE WOODCUTTER. Early next morning she got up and went to their room, and looked at the two of them lying there asleep.

THE STEPMOTHER. She could barely keep her hands from their full red cheeks.

THE WITCH. 'Nice mouthfuls!'

THE WOODCUTTER. she thought.

THE STEPMOTHER. Then she seized Hansel

THE WOODCUTTER. and before he could utter a cry she dragged him out of the cottage and into a little shed, where she shut him in a cage.

The horrific torture chamber is revealed, and HANSEL *is incarcerated.*

THE STEPMOTHER. He cried then all right,

THE WITCH. but there was no one to hear.

THE WOODCUTTER. Then the witch shook Gretel awake saying,

THE WITCH. 'Get up, you lump! Go and fetch some water from the well and cook something for your brother. He's in the shed, and I want him fattened up. When he's fat enough, I'm going to eat him.'

THE WOODCUTTER. Gretel began to cry,

THE STEPMOTHER. but it was no good: she had to do everything the witch ordered.

A daily routine.

GRETEL. Hansel was given delicious food every day,

HANSEL. while she had to live on crayfish shells.

THE WOODCUTTER. Every morning the witch limped down to the shed, leaning on her stick, and said to Hansel:

THE WITCH. 'Boy! Stick your finger out! I want to see if you're fat yet.'

GRETEL. But Hansel was too clever for that: he stuck a little bone through the bars,

HANSEL. and the witch, peering through her red eyes, thought it was his finger.

THE STEPMOTHER. She couldn't understand why he wasn't fat.

THE WOODCUTTER. Four weeks went by, and she thought Hansel was still thin. But then she thought of his nice red cheeks, and she shouted to Gretel:

THE WITCH. 'Hey! Girl! Go and fetch lots of water. Fill the cauldron and set it on to boil. Fat or thin, skinny or plump, I'm going to slaughter that brother of yours tomorrow and boil him up for a stew.'

THE WOODCUTTER. Poor Gretel! She wept and wept,

THE STEPMOTHER. but she had to fetch the water as the witch ordered.

GRETEL (*sobbing*). 'Please, God, help us! If only the wolves had eaten us in the forest, at least we'd have died together.'

THE WITCH. 'Stop your snivelling. It won't do you any good.'

THE STEPMOTHER. In the morning Gretel had to light a fire under the oven.

THE WITCH. 'We'll do the baking first. I've kneaded the dough already. Is that fire hot enough yet?'

THE WOODCUTTER. She dragged Gretel to the oven door.

GRETEL. Flames were spitting and flaring under the iron floor.

THE WITCH. 'Climb in and see if it's hot enough. Go on, in you go.'

THE STEPMOTHER. Of course, the witch intended to shut the door when Gretel was inside, and cook her as well.

THE WOODCUTTER. But Gretel saw what she was up to, so she said,

GRETEL. 'I don't quite understand. You want me to get inside? How can I do that?'

THE WITCH. 'Stupid goose. Get out of the way, I'll show you. It's easy enough.'

GRETEL. And she bent down and put her head inside the oven.

THE STEPMOTHER. As soon as she did, Gretel shoved her so hard that she overbalanced and fell in.

THE WOODCUTTER. Gretel closed the door at once and secured it with an iron bar.

GRETEL. Horrible shrieks and screams and howls came from the oven,

THE WOODCUTTER. but Gretel closed her ears and ran outside.

THE STEPMOTHER. The witch burned to death.

THE WOODCUTTER. Gretel ran straight to the shed and cried:

GRETEL. 'Hansel, we're safe! The old witch is dead!'

THE STEPMOTHER. Hansel leaped out, as joyful as a bird that finds its cage open.

HANSEL. They were so happy!

THE STEPMOTHER. They threw their arms around each other's necks,

THE WOODCUTTER. they hugged,

THE STEPMOTHER. they jumped for joy,

THE WOODCUTTER. they kissed each other's cheeks.

GRETEL. There was nothing to fear any more,

THE STEPMOTHER. so they ran into the cottage and looked around.

GRETEL. In every corner there were trunks and chests full of precious stones.

HANSEL. 'These are better than pebbles!'

THE STEPMOTHER. said Hansel, dropping some in his pocket.

GRETEL. 'I'll take some too,'

THE WOODCUTTER. said Gretel, and filled her apron with them.

HANSEL. 'And now let's go. Let's leave these witchy woods behind.'

THE STEPMOTHER. After walking a few hours, they came to a lake.

HANSEL. 'It's going to be difficult to get across. I can't see a bridge anywhere.'

GRETEL. 'There aren't any boats either. But look – there's a white duck. I'll see if she can help us get across.'

THE WOODCUTTER. She called out:

GRETEL.
'Little duckling, little duck,
Be kind enough to bring us luck!
The water's deep and cold and wide,
And we must reach the other side.'

THE WHITE DUCK. The little duck swam up to them, and Hansel climbed on her back.

HANSEL. 'Come on, Gretel! Climb on with me!'

GRETEL. 'No, that would be too much of a cargo. We should go one at a time.'

THE STEPMOTHER. So the good little bird took them one after the other.

THE WHITE DUCK. When they were safely ashore again they walked on further,

HANSEL. and soon the forest began to grow more familiar.

GRETEL. At last they saw their own home in the distance,

THE WHITE DUCK. and they ran up and rushed inside and threw themselves into their father's arms.

THE WOODCUTTER. The man hadn't had one happy moment since he'd left his children in the forest.

THE WITCH. Not long after that, his wife had died,

THE STEPMOTHER (*bitter, even from beyond the grave*). and he was all alone, and poorer than ever.

HANSEL. But now Gretel unfolded her little apron and shook out all the jewels

THE WOODCUTTER. so that they bounced and scattered all over the room,

GRETEL. and Hansel threw handful after handful after them.

HANSEL. So all their troubles were over,

THE WOODCUTTER. and they lived happily ever after.

A game, to celebrate.

HANSEL.
The mouse has run,

GRETEL.
My tale is done –

THE WITCH.
   And if you catch it,

THE WOODCUTTER.
                   you can make yourself

THE STEPMOTHER.
                           a great big furry hat.

Faithful Johannes

*This truly is an epic Tale, involving vast castles with unending
corridors, perilous voyages over tempestuous seas, talking
ravens, decapitations… As in previous Tales, it is important
that movement between each part is deft. In the original
production,* THE RAVENS, *dressed in tattered black raincoats,
wore half-masks with huge beaks, while puppets ensured that
the sacrifice of* THE PRINCES *was suitably horrific.*

Prologue: a formal procession, accompanied by music, as
THE OLD KING *shuffles towards his bed – his final resting
place – followed by his anxious court. Then…*

THE PRINCESS. Once upon a time

THE YOUNG KING. there was an old king who fell ill,

THE FIRST SERVANT. and as he was lying in pain he thought,

THE OLD KING. 'This bed I'm lying on will be my deathbed.'

THE SECOND SERVANT. And he said,

THE OLD KING. 'Send for Faithful Johannes – I want to speak
to him.'

THE FIRST SERVANT. Faithful Johannes was his favourite
servant.

JOHANNES. He had that name because he'd been true and
loyal to the king all his life long.

THE SECOND SERVANT. When he came into the king's
bedroom the king beckoned him close to the bed, and said,

THE OLD KING. 'My good and faithful Johannes, I'm not
long for this world. The only thing that troubles me is my
son. He's a good lad, but he's young, and he doesn't always
know what's best for him. I won't be able to close my eyes
in peace unless you promise to be like a foster father to him,
and teach him all he ought to know.'

THE PRINCESS. Faithful Johannes said,

JOHANNES. 'I'll do that gladly. I won't forsake him, and I'll serve him faithfully even if it costs me my life.'

THE OLD KING. 'That's a comfort to me. I can die peacefully now. When I've gone, this is what you must do: show him over the whole castle, all the vaults, the chambers, the halls, and all the treasure they contain. But keep him away from the last room in the long gallery. There's a portrait of the Princess of the Golden Roof in there, and if he sees that picture, he'll fall in love with her. You'll know if that's happened, because he'll fall down unconscious. And then he'll put himself into all kinds of dangers for her sake. Keep him away from all that, Johannes: that's the last thing I ask of you.'

JOHANNES. Faithful Johannes gave his promise,

THE FIRST SERVANT. and the old king lay back on his pillow

THE YOUNG KING. and died.

JOHANNES *gently brushes his hand over* THE OLD KING*'s face, to close the dead man's eyes.*

THE PRINCESS. After the funeral, Faithful Johannes said to the young king,

JOHANNES. 'It's time you saw all your possessions, your majesty. Your father asked me to show you over the castle. It belongs to you now, and you need to know about all the treasures it holds.'

A tour, during which THE YOUNG KING *meets various members of the royal household.*

THE YOUNG KING. Johannes took him everywhere,

THE FIRST SERVANT. upstairs and downstairs,

THE FOURTH SERVANT. up in the attics

THE SECOND SERVANT. and way below ground in the cellars.

THE YOUNG KING. All the magnificent rooms were open to him –

The ghost of THE OLD KING *watches over his wayward son – but is unable to intervene.*

THE OLD KING. all but one, that is,

JOHANNES. because Faithful Johannes kept the young king away from the last room in the long gallery,

THE PRINCESS. where the portrait of the Princess of the Golden Roof was hung.

THE SECOND SERVANT. The picture was displayed in such a way that anyone entering the room would see it at once,

THE FIRST SERVANT. and it was painted so well and so vividly that the princess seemed to live and breathe.

JOHANNES. No one could imagine anything in the world more beautiful.

THE OLD KING. The king noticed that Faithful Johannes always ushered him past that door, or tried to distract him when they were near it, and said,

THE YOUNG KING. 'Come on, Johannes, I can see you're trying to stop me going in there. Why do you never open this door?'

JOHANNES. 'There's something horrifying in there, your majesty. You don't want to see it.'

THE YOUNG KING. 'I certainly do! I've seen the whole castle now, and this is the last room. I want to know what's in it!'

THE FIRST SERVANT. And he tried to open the door by force,

THE SECOND SERVANT. but Faithful Johannes held him back.

JOHANNES. 'I promised the king your father that I wouldn't let you see inside this room. It will bring nothing but bad luck for both of us.'

THE YOUNG KING. 'Well, you're wrong about that. I'm so curious to see what's inside, it'll be bad luck if I can't. I shall have no peace, day or night, till I know what's in there. Johannes, open the door!'

THE OLD KING. Faithful Johannes saw that he had no choice.

THE SECOND SERVANT. With a heavy heart and sighing deeply,

THE FIRST SERVANT. he took the key from the ring

THE OLD KING. and opened the door.

JOHANNES *enters the room, in which the portrait of* THE PRINCESS *is covered with a dustsheet.* THE SERVANTS *peep through the door.*

THE YOUNG KING. He went in first,

JOHANNES. thinking that he might block the portrait from the young king's eyes,

THE FIRST SERVANT. but that didn't work:

THE SECOND SERVANT. the king stood on tiptoes and looked over his shoulder.

THE OLD KING. And it happened just as the old king had said it would:

The dustsheet drops, revealing THE PRINCESS *standing in a sumptuous gilt frame.*

THE FIRST SERVANT. the young man saw the portrait,

JOHANNES. and at once he fell unconscious to the floor.

THE SECOND SERVANT. Faithful Johannes picked him up and carried him to his room.

JOHANNES. 'Oh, Lord – this is a bad start to his reign. What bad luck will come to us now?'

THE FIRST SERVANT. The king soon came back to his senses, however, and said,

THE YOUNG KING. 'What a beautiful picture! What a beautiful girl! Who is she?'

JOHANNES. 'She's the Princess of the Golden Roof.'

THE YOUNG KING. 'Oh, I'm in love, Johannes! I love her so much that if all the leaves on all the trees were tongues, they couldn't express it. I'd risk my life to win her love. Johannes, my faithful servant, you must help me! How can we reach her?'

THE OLD KING. Faithful Johannes thought hard about this.

JOHANNES. It was well known that the princess was a reclusive character.

THE SECOND SERVANT. However, he soon thought of a plan, and went to tell the king.

JOHANNES. 'Everything she has around her is gold: tables, chairs, dishes, sofas, knives and forks, all solid gold. Now among your treasures, your majesty, as you'll no doubt remember, are five tonnes of gold. What I suggest is to get the royal goldsmiths to take, say, a tonne of it and make all manner of pretty things, birds and beasts and strange animals and the like. They might take her fancy, and we could try our luck.'

THE THIRD GOLDSMITH. The king summoned all the goldsmiths

THE YOUNG KING. and told them what he wanted.

THE FIRST GOLDSMITH. They worked night and day

THE SECOND GOLDSMITH. and produced a large number of pieces so beautiful

THE THIRD GOLDSMITH. that the young king was sure the princess would never have seen the like.

A SAILOR. They loaded everything on board a ship,

JOHANNES. and Faithful Johannes and the king disguised themselves as merchants

THE YOUNG KING. so that they were quite unrecognisable.

THE BOSUN. Then they weighed anchor, and they sailed across the sea

A brief moment, to mark this long journey.

THE YOUNG KING. until they came to the city of the Princess of the Golden Roof.

A SAILOR. Faithful Johannes said to the king,

JOHANNES. 'I think you should wait on the ship, your majesty. I'll go ashore and see if I can interest the princess in our gold. What you'd best do is set some things out for her to look at. Decorate the ship a bit.'

THE BOSUN. The king set to eagerly,

A SAILOR. and Faithful Johannes went ashore with some of the smaller gold objects in his apron,

THE YOUNG KING. and went straight to the palace.

THE YOUNG KING, THE SAILOR *and* THE BOSUN *watch the encounter that follows from on board ship, through telescopes.*

THE PRINCESS. In the courtyard he found

JOHANNES. a beautiful girl drawing water from two wells with two golden buckets,

A SAILOR. one for plain water

THE BOSUN. and one for sparkling.

JOHANNES. She was about to turn and go in

THE CHAMBERMAID. when she saw Faithful Johannes and asked who he was.

JOHANNES. 'I'm a merchant. I've come from a far land to see if anyone's interested in our gold.'

A SAILOR. He opened his apron to show her.

THE CHAMBERMAID. 'Oh, what lovely things!'

THE BOSUN. she said,

THE YOUNG KING. putting the buckets down and taking up the gold pieces one after the other.

THE CHAMBERMAID. 'I must tell the princess about them. She loves gold, you know, and I'm sure she'd buy everything you've got.'

THE YOUNG KING. She took Faithful Johannes by the hand, and led him upstairs,

THE CHAMBERMAID. for she was the princess's own chambermaid.

JOHANNES. When the princess saw the golden objects she was delighted.

THE PRINCESS. 'I've never seen such beautifully made things. I can't resist them. Name your price! I'll buy them all.'

A SAILOR. Faithful Johannes said,

JOHANNES. 'Well, your royal highness, I'm only the servant really. My master is the merchant – he usually deals with that side of things. And these little samples of mine aren't to be compared with what he's got on the ship. They're the most beautiful things that have ever been made in gold.'

THE PRINCESS. 'Bring them all here!'

JOHANNES. 'Ah, well, I'd like to oblige you, but there's so many of them. It would take days to bring them all up here, and besides, it would need so much space to set all the pieces out that I don't think your palace has got enough rooms, big and splendid though it is.'

THE YOUNG KING. He thought that would make her curious,

THE CHAMBERMAID. and he was right, because she said,

THE PRINCESS. 'Then I'll come to your ship. Take me there now, and I'll look at all your master's treasures.'

THE BOSUN. Faithful Johannes led her to the ship, feeling very pleased.

THE YOUNG KING. When the young king saw the princess on the quayside, he realised that she was even more beautiful than her portrait, and his heart nearly burst.

THE BOSUN. But he escorted her on board and led her below,

A SAILOR. while Faithful Johannes remained on deck.

JOHANNES (*to* THE BOSUN). 'Cast off and set all the sail you have. Fly like a bird in the air.'

THE YOUNG KING. Meanwhile below decks the king was showing the princess the golden vessels and all the other beautiful objects,

THE PRINCESS. the birds,

THE YOUNG KING. the animals,

THE PRINCESS. the trees and flowers,

THE YOUNG KING. both realistic and fantastical.

A SAILOR. Hours went by,

JOHANNES. and she didn't notice that they were sailing.

THE YOUNG KING. When she'd seen everything she gave a little sigh of contentment.

THE PRINCESS. 'Thank you, sir. What a beautiful collection! I've never seen anything like it. Truly exquisite! But it's time I went home.'

THE BOSUN. And then she looked through the porthole,

THE YOUNG KING. and saw that they were on the high seas.

THE PRINCESS. 'What are you doing? Where are we? I've been betrayed! To fall into the hands of a merchant – but you can't be a merchant! You must be a pirate! Have you kidnapped me? Oh, I'd rather die!'

JOHANNES. The king took her hand and said,

THE YOUNG KING. 'I'm not a merchant. I'm a king, just as well born as you are. If I tricked you into coming on board, it's only because I was overpowered by love. When I saw your portrait in my palace, I fell to the ground unconscious.'

JOHANNES. The Princess of the Golden Roof was reassured by his gentle manner,

THE YOUNG KING. and presently her heart was moved,

THE PRINCESS. and she agreed to become his wife.

A SAILOR. Now as the ship sailed onwards, Faithful Johannes happened to be sitting in the bows, playing the fiddle.

THE YOUNG KING. While he was doing that, three ravens flew around the ship and settled on the bowsprit,

THE PRINCESS. and he stopped playing

JOHANNES. and listened to what they were saying, for he knew the language of the birds. The first said,

THE FIRST RAVEN. 'Kraak! Look! That's the Princess of the Golden Roof! He's taking her home with him!'

JOHANNES. The second one said,

THE SECOND RAVEN. 'Yes, but he hasn't got her yet.'

JOHANNES. The third one said,

THE THIRD RAVEN. 'Yes, he has! Kraak! There she is, sitting next to him on the deck.'

THE FIRST RAVEN. 'That won't do him any good. As soon as they step ashore, a chestnut horse will run up to greet them, and the prince will try and mount it. Kraak! But if he does, the horse will leap into the air and carry him away, and he'll never see her again.'

THE SECOND RAVEN. 'Kraak! Isn't there any way of preventing that?'

THE FIRST RAVEN. 'Yes, of course there is, but they don't know it. If someone else jumps in the saddle, takes the pistol from the holster and shoots the horse dead, the king will be safe. Kraak! But whoever does that must never tell the king why he did it, because if he does, he'll be turned to stone up to his knees.'

THE SECOND RAVEN. 'I know more than that. Even if the horse is killed, the king isn't safe. When they go into the palace, they'll find a beautiful wedding robe laid out for him on a golden tray. It'll seem to be made of gold and silver, but really it's made of sulphur and pitch, and if he puts it on it'll burn his flesh away right down to the marrow. Kraak!'

THE THIRD RAVEN. 'Surely they won't be able to save him from that.'

THE SECOND RAVEN. 'Oh, yes, it's easy, but they don't know how. Someone wearing gloves will have to take the robe and throw it on the fire, and then it'll burn up safely and the king won't be harmed. Kraak! But if he tells the king why he did it, he'll be turned to stone from his knees to his heart.'

THE THIRD RAVEN. 'What a fate! And the dangers don't end there, either. Even if the robe burns up, I don't think this king is destined to have his bride. After the ceremony, when the dancing begins, the young queen will suddenly turn pale and fall down as though dead.'

THE FIRST RAVEN. 'And can she be saved?'

THE THIRD RAVEN. 'With the greatest of ease, if anyone knew. All they have to do is lift her up, bite her right breast, draw three drops of blood from it and spit them out. Then she'll come to life again. But if they tell the king why they've done it, their entire body will turn to stone, from the crown of their head to the soles of their feet. Kraak!'

JOHANNES. And then the ravens flew away.

THE FIRST RAVEN (*with a final look back*). Faithful Johannes had understood every word,

THE YOUNG KING. and from then on he grew silent

THE PRINCESS. and sorrowful.

JOHANNES. If he didn't do what the ravens had said, his master would die, and yet if he explained to the king why he'd done these strange things, he would be turned to stone.

A SAILOR. But finally he said to himself,

JOHANNES. 'Well, he's my master, and I'll save his life even if I have to give up my life in doing so.'

THE OLD KING. When they landed, it happened exactly as the raven had said it would.

THE PRINCESS. A magnificent chestnut horse came galloping up, saddled and bridled in gold.

THE YOUNG KING. 'A good omen! He can carry me to the palace.'

THE FIRST SERVANT. And he was about to climb into the saddle when Faithful Johannes pushed him aside and leaped up himself.

THE YOUNG KING. A moment later he'd pulled out the pistol from the saddle holster

THE PRINCESS. and shot the horse dead.

THE SECOND SERVANT. The king's other servants didn't care much for Johannes,

THE THIRD SERVANT. and they said,

THE FIRST SERVANT. 'What a shame to kill such a beautiful horse!

THE SECOND SERVANT. And to shove the king aside like that, what's more,

THE THIRD SERVANT. just as it was going to carry him to the palace.'

THE YOUNG KING. 'Hold your tongues. This is Faithful Johannes you're talking about. I'm sure he had a good reason for it.'

THE SECOND SERVANT. They went into the palace,

THE PRINCESS. and there in the hall was a beautiful robe laid out on a golden tray,

JOHANNES. just as the raven had said.

THE THIRD SERVANT. Faithful Johannes was watching closely,

THE PRINCESS. and as soon as the king moved to pick it up,

THE FIRST SERVANT. Johannes pulled his gloves on,

THE SECOND SERVANT. snatched the robe away,

THE THIRD SERVANT. and threw it on the fire.

THE YOUNG KING. It blazed up fiercely.

JOHANNES. The other servants whispered together again:

THE THIRD SERVANT. 'See that?

THE SECOND SERVANT. See what he did?

THE FIRST SERVANT. He burned the king's wedding robe!'

THE THIRD SERVANT. But the young king said,

THE YOUNG KING. 'Enough of that! I'm sure Johannes had a good reason. Leave him alone.'

THE PRINCESS. Then the wedding took place.

A brief ceremony, presided over by THE PRIEST.

THE FIRST SERVANT. After the service the dancing began,

THE THIRD SERVANT. and Faithful Johannes stood at the edge of the ballroom,

JOHANNES. never taking his eyes off the queen.

THE YOUNG KING. Suddenly she turned pale and fell to the floor.

THE FIRST SERVANT. At once Johannes ran to her, picked her up, and carried her to the royal bedchamber.

THE SECOND SERVANT. He laid her down, and then knelt and first bit her right breast

THE THIRD SERVANT. and then sucked out three drops of blood,

THE FIRST SERVANT. and spat them out.

THE THIRD SERVANT. Instantly she opened her eyes and looked around,

THE QUEEN. and then sat up, breathing easily,

JOHANNES. perfectly well again.

THE YOUNG KING. The king had seen everything,

THE FIRST SERVANT. and not understanding why Johannes had behaved like that, became angry and ordered the guards to

THE YOUNG KING. take him to prison at once.

An ominous drumbeat: a march to the scaffold.

THE THIRD SERVANT. Next morning Faithful Johannes was condemned to death and led to the gallows.

THE HANGMAN. As he stood on the scaffold with the noose around his neck he said,

JOHANNES. 'Everyone condemned to die is allowed to say one last thing. Do I also have the right?'

THE YOUNG KING. 'Yes. You have that right.'

JOHANNES. 'I've been unjustly condemned. I've always been loyal to you, your majesty, just as I was to your father.'

THE SECOND SERVANT. And he told all about the conversation between the ravens on the bowsprit,

THE HANGMAN. and how he had to do these strange things in order to save the king and queen from death.

THE FIRST SERVANT. Hearing that, the king cried out,

THE YOUNG KING. 'Oh, my Faithful Johannes! A pardon! A pardon for you! Bring him down at once!'

THE QUEEN. But something strange was happening to Johannes:

JOHANNES. as he spoke the very last word,

JOHANNES' *body is wrapped in bandages, like a mummification.*

THE FIRST SERVANT. his feet

THE SECOND SERVANT. and then his legs

THE THIRD SERVANT. and then his trunk and his arms

THE QUEEN. and finally his head

THE YOUNG KING. changed into stone.

And JOHANNES *is indeed now a* STONE FIGURE.

THE FIRST SERVANT. The king and the queen were grief-stricken.

THE YOUNG KING. 'Oh, what a terrible reward for his loyalty to us!'

THE SECOND SERVANT. the king said,

THE THIRD SERVANT. and he ordered the stone figure to be carried to his bedchamber

THE FIRST SERVANT. and placed next to his bed.

THE QUEEN. Every time he looked at it, the tears flowed down his cheeks, and he'd say,

THE YOUNG KING. 'Oh, if only I could bring you back to life, my dear, most faithful Johannes!'

The ghost of THE OLD KING *reappears in the royal bedchamber, to witness how his son redeems himself.*

THE OLD KING. Time went by, and the queen gave birth

Two STORYTELLERS *present the puppet* PRINCES.

THE TWO PRINCES. to twin boys,

THE QUEEN. who were healthy and happy and became her
greatest delight.

THE OLD KING. One day when the queen was at church,
the two boys were playing in their father's bedroom,

THE FIRST PRINCE. and their father the king looked at the
stone figure

THE SECOND PRINCE. and said, as he always did,

THE YOUNG KING. 'Oh, my dear faithful Johannes, if only
I could bring you back to life!'

THE OLD KING. And then to his astonishment the stone began
to speak and said,

THE STONE FIGURE. 'You can bring me back to life, if you
sacrifice what you love most.'

THE OLD KING. The king said,

THE YOUNG KING. 'For you I'll give up everything I have!'

THE OLD KING. The stone went on,

THE STONE FIGURE. 'If you cut off your children's heads
with your own hand and sprinkle their blood on me, I shall
come back to life.'

THE OLD KING. The king was horrified. To kill his own
beloved children! What a terrible price to pay!

THE YOUNG KING. But he remembered how Faithful
Johannes had been ready to give his own life for those
he served,

THE OLD KING. and he steeled himself,

THE YOUNG KING. drew his sword,

THE OLD KING. and lopped off his two children's heads in
a moment.

The STORYTELLERS *step back, shocked, from the
decapitated bodies of* THE PRINCES, *before they assist in
the demummification of* JOHANNES.

THE FIRST PRINCE. And when he had sprinkled the stone figure with their blood,

THE SECOND PRINCE. the stone changed into flesh again,

THE FIRST PRINCE. starting at the head

THE SECOND PRINCE. and going all the way down to the toes,

THE YOUNG KING. and there was Faithful Johannes, healthy and well.

THE OLD KING. He said to the king,

JOHANNES. 'You were faithful to me, your majesty, and you won't go unrewarded.'

THE YOUNG KING. And Johannes took the children's heads

THE FIRST PRINCE. and put them on again,

. THE SECOND PRINCE. rubbing their necks with their own blood,

The STORYTELLERS *bring* THE PRINCES *back to life again.*

THE FIRST PRINCE. and they sat up

THE SECOND PRINCE. and blinked

JOHANNES. and came alive once more,

THE YOUNG KING. and went on jumping around and playing as if nothing had happened.

THE OLD KING. The king was overjoyed.

THE SECOND PRINCE. And then he heard the queen coming back from church,

THE FIRST PRINCE. and he made Johannes and the children

THE YOUNG KING. hide in the wardrobe.

THE OLD KING. When she came in, he said,

THE YOUNG KING. 'My dear, have you been praying?'

THE QUEEN. 'Yes – but my mind was always on Faithful Johannes and what a dreadful thing happened to him because of us.'

THE YOUNG KING. 'Well, we can bring him back to life, but it'll be at a heavy cost. We shall have to sacrifice our two little boys.'

THE OLD KING. The queen turned pale,

THE QUEEN. and horror nearly stopped her heart.

THE OLD KING. But she said,

THE QUEEN. 'We owe him that much, for his great loyalty.'

THE YOUNG KING. The king rejoiced to hear that her response was the same as his,

THE OLD KING. and he opened the wardrobe

JOHANNES. and out came Faithful Johannes

THE TWO PRINCES. and the two little boys.

THE YOUNG KING. 'God be praised! Faithful Johannes has been saved, and our two sons are alive as well!'

THE QUEEN. He told the queen how everything had come about.

THE OLD KING. And after that they lived together happily

JOHANNES. till the end of their lives.

And finally, THE OLD KING *is able to rest in peace.*

The Donkey Cabbage

This Tale includes another enchanted forest – but is less about this place than it is about magic. There's heart-swallowing and some A Midsummer Night's Dream-*style donkey transformations to negotiate, along with an encounter with three* GIANTS – *and a magic-carpet ride on a cloud!*

THE WITCH. There was once

THE YOUNG HUNTER. a young hunter

THE HUNTER'S FATHER. who went out to his hide in the forest.

THE HUNTER'S MOTHER. He was happy and light-hearted,

THE DAUGHTER. and he whistled on a blade of grass as he went along.

THE HUNTER'S FATHER. All at once

THE YOUNG HUNTER. he came across a poor old woman.

THE HUNTER'S MOTHER. She said,

THE OLD WOMAN. 'Good morning, my fine young hunter. I can see you're in a good mood, but I'm hungry and thirsty. Can you spare me any change?'

THE DAUGHTER. The hunter felt sorry for the old woman,

THE HUNTER'S FATHER. so he put his hand in his pocket

THE YOUNG HUNTER. and gave her the few coins he had.

THE HUNTER'S MOTHER. He was about to go on his way

THE YOUNG HUNTER. when the old woman clutched his arm.

THE OLD WOMAN. 'Listen, my good hunter. You've been kind to me, so I'm going to give you a gift. Carry straight on, and in a little while you'll come to a tree with nine birds sitting in it. They'll have a cloak in their claws, and they'll be fighting over it. Take your gun and shoot right into the middle of them. They'll drop the cloak all right, and one of the birds will fall dead at your feet. Take the cloak with you, because it's a wishing cloak. Once you throw it round your shoulders, all you've got to do is wish yourself somewhere, and you'll be there in a flash. And you should take the heart from the dead bird, too. Cut it out and then swallow it whole. If you do that, you'll find a gold coin under your pillow every morning of your life.'

THE HUNTER'S MOTHER. The hunter thanked the wise woman

THE HUNTER'S FATHER. and thought to himself:

THE YOUNG HUNTER. 'These are certainly fine gifts she's giving me; I hope she's telling the truth.'

THE DAUGHTER. He'd gone no further than a hundred yards

THE HUNTER'S MOTHER. when he heard a great squawking and flapping in the branches above him.

THE HUNTER'S FATHER. He looked up and saw a flock of birds

THE YOUNG HUNTER. all tearing at a piece of cloth with their claws and beaks,

THE WITCH. as if each one wanted it for itself.

THE YOUNG HUNTER. 'Well, this is odd. It's happening just as the old girl said it would.'

THE HUNTER'S FATHER. He took his gun

THE HUNTER'S MOTHER. and fired a shot

THE YOUNG HUNTER. right into the middle of the birds.

THE DAUGHTER. Most of them shrieked and flew away at once,

THE WITCH. but one fell to the ground dead,

THE YOUNG HUNTER. and the cloak fell too.

THE HUNTER'S MOTHER. The hunter did just as the old woman had advised.

THE HUNTER'S FATHER. He cut the bird open with his knife,

THE YOUNG HUNTER. took out the heart

THE WITCH. and swallowed it,

THE DAUGHTER. and went home with the cloak.

THE HUNTER'S MOTHER. When he woke up next morning,

THE YOUNG HUNTER. the first thing he thought of was the old woman's promise.

THE HUNTER'S FATHER. He felt under his pillow,

THE YOUNG HUNTER. and sure enough, there was a gleaming gold coin.

THE DAUGHTER. Next day he found another one,

THE YOUNG HUNTER. and then another,

THE DAUGHTER. and so it went on each time he woke up.

THE WITCH. Quite soon he had a fine heap of gold,

THE DAUGHTER. and then he thought,

THE YOUNG HUNTER. 'It's all very well collecting this, but what use is it to me here? I think I'll go out and see the world.'

THE WITCH. He said

THE YOUNG HUNTER. goodbye

THE WITCH. to his parents,

THE HUNTER'S FATHER. slung his gun

THE HUNTER'S MOTHER. and his knapsack

THE DAUGHTER. over his shoulders,

THE YOUNG HUNTER. and set off.

THE HUNTER'S MOTHER. After walking for a few days,

THE HUNTER'S FATHER. he was just coming out of a dense forest

THE HUNTER'S MOTHER. when he saw

THE YOUNG HUNTER. a beautiful castle standing in the open country beyond the trees.

THE HUNTER'S FATHER. He went closer, and saw

THE HUNTER'S MOTHER. two people standing at one of the windows,

THE YOUNG HUNTER. looking down at him.

THE HUNTER'S FATHER. One of them was an old woman,

THE HUNTER'S MOTHER. and she was a witch.

THE HUNTER'S FATHER. She said to the other,

THE HUNTER'S MOTHER. who was her daughter,

THE WITCH. 'That man who's just coming out of the forest has got a great treasure inside him. We must get it for ourselves, my honey, because we can make much better use of it than he's doing. You see, he swallowed the heart of a particular bird, and as a result he finds a gold coin under his pillow every morning.'

THE HUNTER'S FATHER. She went on to tell her daughter the whole story of the hunter and the wise woman,

THE DAUGHTER. and she finished by saying,

THE WITCH. 'And if you don't do exactly as I tell you, my dear, you'll be sorry.'

THE HUNTER'S MOTHER. As the hunter came closer to the castle he saw them more clearly,

THE HUNTER'S FATHER. and thought,

THE YOUNG HUNTER. 'I've been wandering about for quite a while now, and I've got plenty of money. Maybe I'll stop at this castle for a day or two and have a rest.'

THE WITCH. Of course, the real reason was that the girl was very beautiful.

THE HUNTER'S MOTHER. He went into the castle,

THE DAUGHTER. where they welcomed him

THE WITCH. and looked after him generously.

THE HUNTER'S FATHER. Before long he was in love with the witch's daughter,

THE YOUNG HUNTER. so much so that he could think of nothing else;

THE WITCH. he had eyes only for her,

THE DAUGHTER. and whatever she wanted him to do, he did.

THE YOUNG HUNTER. In fact he was besotted.

THE HUNTER'S MOTHER. Seeing this, the old woman said to the girl,

THE WITCH. 'This is the time to act. We've got to get that bird's heart. He won't even notice it's gone.'

THE DAUGHTER. She prepared a potion,

THE HUNTER'S FATHER. and poured it into a cup

THE WITCH. for the girl to hand to the young man.

THE DAUGHTER. 'My dearest one, won't you drink to my health?'

THE WITCH. He drank it all down in one,

THE HUNTER'S MOTHER. and almost immediately he was so sick

THE DAUGHTER. that he vomited up the bird's heart.

THE HUNTER'S FATHER. The girl helped him to lie down,

THE YOUNG HUNTER. with many soft words of concern,

THE HUNTER'S MOTHER. and then went straight back,

THE DAUGHTER. found the heart,

THE HUNTER'S FATHER. rinsed it in clean water

THE WITCH. and swallowed it herself.

THE HUNTER'S MOTHER. From then on the hunter found no more gold coins under his pillow.

THE HUNTER'S FATHER. He had no idea that they were appearing under the girl's,

THE DAUGHTER. and that the witch collected them every morning

THE WITCH. and hid them away.

THE HUNTER'S MOTHER. He was so infatuated that

THE YOUNG HUNTER. all he wanted to do was spend time with her daughter.

THE HUNTER'S FATHER. The witch said,

THE WITCH. 'We've got the heart, but that isn't enough. We must have the wishing cloak too.'

THE DAUGHTER. 'Can't we leave him that? After all, the poor man's lost his fortune.'

THE WITCH. 'Don't you be so soft! A cloak like that is worth millions. There aren't many of them about, I can tell you. I must have it, and I will have it.'

THE HUNTER'S MOTHER. She told her daughter what to do

THE DAUGHTER. and said that if she didn't obey, she'd regret it.

THE HUNTER'S FATHER. So the girl did as the witch said:

THE HUNTER'S MOTHER. she stood at the window gazing out

THE WITCH. as if she were very sad.

THE HUNTER'S FATHER. The hunter said,

THE YOUNG HUNTER. 'Why are you standing there looking so sad?'

THE DAUGHTER. 'Ah, my treasure, out there lies Mount Garnet, where the most precious jewels grow. When I think of them I want them so much that I can't help feeling sad... But who can go there and gather them? Only the birds, who can fly. I'm sure a human being could never get there.'

THE YOUNG HUNTER. 'If that's all that's troubling you, leave it to me. I'll soon cheer you up.'

THE HUNTER'S MOTHER. He took his cloak and swung it around his shoulders,

THE YOUNG HUNTER. and over her as well,

THE DAUGHTER. so it enfolded both of them.

THE WITCH. Then he wished to be on Mount Garnet.

THE HUNTER'S FATHER. The blink of an eye later,

THE YOUNG HUNTER. they were sitting near the top of it.

THE DAUGHTER. Precious stones of every kind sparkled
brilliantly all around them;

THE YOUNG HUNTER. they had never seen anything
so lovely.

THE WITCH. However, the witch had cast a spell

THE HUNTER'S MOTHER. to make the hunter sleepy,

THE HUNTER'S FATHER. and he said to the girl,

THE YOUNG HUNTER. 'Let's sit down and rest a while. I'm
so tired my legs can't keep me up.'

THE HUNTER'S MOTHER. They sat down,

THE DAUGHTER. he laid his head in her lap,

THE WITCH. and a moment later his eyes began to close.

THE HUNTER'S FATHER. As soon as he was fast asleep,

THE HUNTER'S MOTHER. she took the cloak from around
his shoulders and wrapped it around herself,

THE WITCH. before gathering as many garnets and other
jewels as she could carry

THE DAUGHTER. and wishing herself back home.

THE HUNTER'S MOTHER. When the hunter awoke

THE HUNTER'S FATHER. and found himself alone on the
wild mountain,

THE YOUNG HUNTER. and that his cloak had gone too,

THE WITCH. he realised that his beloved had deceived him.

THE YOUNG HUNTER. 'Oh. I didn't know the world was so
full of treachery!'

THE HUNTER'S MOTHER. He sat there too distressed
to move.

THE HUNTER'S FATHER. He couldn't think what to do.

THE DAUGHTER. Now the mountain happened to belong to some ferocious giants,

THE WITCH. great thundering brutes,

THE HUNTER'S MOTHER. and it wasn't long before the hunter heard three of them coming.

THE HUNTER'S FATHER. He lay down quickly

THE YOUNG HUNTER. and pretended to be fast asleep.

THE SECOND GIANT. The first giant prodded him with his toe and said,

THE FIRST GIANT. 'What's this earthworm doing here?'

THE SECOND GIANT. 'Squash him,'

THE THIRD GIANT. said the second.

THE SECOND GIANT. 'I would.'

THE FIRST GIANT. But the third one said,

THE THIRD GIANT 'Don't bother. There's nothing here for him to live on, so he'll be dead soon in any case. Besides, if he climbs to the top, the clouds will carry him away.'

THE FIRST GIANT. They left him alone

THE SECOND GIANT. and carried on talking

THE THIRD GIANT. as they walked off.

THE WITCH. The hunter had heard everything they'd said,

THE YOUNG HUNTER. and as soon as they were out of sight,

THE WITCH. he got to his feet and clambered up the mountain to the peak,

THE YOUNG HUNTER. which was surrounded by clouds.

Three STORYTELLERS *buffet* THE YOUNG HUNTER *with pillows.*

THE HUNTER'S MOTHER. He sat down on the jewelled pinnacle,

THE YOUNG HUNTER. while clouds came and bumped into him,

THE HUNTER'S FATHER. and finally one of them grabbed him

THE DAUGHTER. and tossed him on board.

THE HUNTER'S MOTHER. It floated around the sky for some time,

THE YOUNG HUNTER. and very comfortable it was too,

THE WITCH. and the hunter saw many interesting things as he peered over the side;

THE HUNTER'S FATHER. but eventually

THE YOUNG HUNTER. it began to sink towards the ground,

THE DAUGHTER. and soon enough he was deposited in someone's kitchen garden,

THE YOUNG HUNTER. which had high walls around it.

THE WITCH. The cloud floated up again

THE HUNTER'S MOTHER. and left him standing

THE HUNTER'S FATHER. between the cabbages and the onions.

THE YOUNG HUNTER. 'Pity there's no fruit,'

THE DAUGHTER. he said to himself.

THE YOUNG HUNTER. 'I wouldn't mind a nice apple or a pear, and I'm so hungry. Still, I can always have a mouthful of cabbage. It doesn't taste wonderful, but it'll keep me going.'

THE WITCH. There were two kinds of cabbages growing in the garden,

THE HUNTER'S MOTHER. pointed ones

THE HUNTER'S FATHER. and round ones,

THE DAUGHTER. and to begin with the hunter pulled a few leaves off a pointed one

THE WITCH. and started to chew.

THE YOUNG HUNTER. It tasted good enough,

THE DAUGHTER. but when he'd only had a few bites,

THE YOUNG HUNTER. he felt the strangest sensation:

THE HUNTER'S FATHER. his skin tickled all over

THE YOUNG HUNTER. as long hairs sprouted out of it,

THE HUNTER'S MOTHER. his spine bent forward

THE YOUNG HUNTER. and his arms lengthened

THE WITCH. and turned into hairy legs

THE YOUNG HUNTER. with hooves on the ends of them,

THE DAUGHTER. his neck thickened

THE YOUNG HUNTER. and grew longer,

THE HUNTER'S FATHER. his face lengthened

THE YOUNG HUNTER. and two long ears shot up from the sides of his head,

THE HUNTER'S MOTHER. and before he knew what was happening, he was

THE YOUNG HUNTER (*braying*). a don-key.

THE WITCH. Needless to say, that made the cabbage taste much better.

THE DAUGHTER. He went on eating it with relish,

THE YOUNG HUNTER. and then moved on to a round cabbage.

THE HUNTER'S FATHER. He'd only had a couple of bites

THE HUNTER'S MOTHER. when he found it all happening again,

THE YOUNG HUNTER. but in reverse,

THE WITCH. and in less time than it takes to tell it,

THE DAUGHTER. he was a human being again.

THE YOUNG HUNTER. 'Well, how about that? Now I can get back what belongs to me.'

THE HUNTER'S FATHER. So he picked a head of the pointed cabbage

THE YOUNG HUNTER. and a head of the round one,

THE HUNTER'S MOTHER. put them safely in his knapsack,

THE HUNTER'S FATHER. and climbed the wall

THE YOUNG HUNTER. and got away.

THE HUNTER'S MOTHER. He soon discovered where he was,

THE HUNTER'S FATHER. and set off back to the castle where the witch lived.

THE HUNTER'S MOTHER. After some days' walking he found it again,

THE HUNTER'S FATHER. and kept out of sight

THE YOUNG HUNTER. while he dyed his face so brown

THE HUNTER'S MOTHER. that even his own mother wouldn't have recognised him.

THE DAUGHTER. Then he knocked at the door.

Knock knock knock.

THE HUNTER'S FATHER. The witch herself opened it.

THE YOUNG HUNTER. 'Can you give me shelter for the night?'

THE HUNTER'S MOTHER. the young man said.

THE YOUNG HUNTER. 'I'm worn out, and I can't go any further.'

THE WITCH. 'Who are you, my dear? What brings you out this way?'

THE YOUNG HUNTER. 'I'm a royal messenger, and the king sent me specially to look for the most delicious cabbage in the world. I was lucky enough to find it, and it really is delicious, but the weather's been so hot that it's beginning to wilt. I don't think I'll get it back in time.'

THE DAUGHTER. When the witch heard about this delicious cabbage, she couldn't wait to try it herself.

THE WITCH. 'Have you got a little bit my daughter and I could taste?'

THE YOUNG HUNTER. 'I brought two heads of it. I don't see why you shouldn't have one of them, since you're being kind enough to let me stay the night.'

THE HUNTER'S FATHER. He opened his knapsack

THE HUNTER'S MOTHER. and gave her the donkey cabbage.

THE DAUGHTER. She took it eagerly and hurried to the kitchen,

THE WITCH. her mouth already watering.

THE HUNTER'S FATHER. She put some water on to boil

THE WITCH. and chopped the cabbage up daintily,

THE HUNTER'S MOTHER. and boiled it for just a few minutes

THE WITCH. with some salt and a little butter.

THE YOUNG HUNTER. It smelt so good that she couldn't resist,

THE DAUGHTER. and before she brought it to the table she nibbled at one of the leaves,

THE WITCH. and then another,

THE HUNTER'S FATHER. and of course as soon as she swallowed them

THE HUNTER'S MOTHER. she started to change.

THE DAUGHTER. In a matter of seconds she was

THE WITCH. an *ee*-old donkey,

THE YOUNG HUNTER. and she ran out into the courtyard to kick up her heels.

THE HUNTER'S FATHER. Next the serving girl came in,

THE YOUNG HUNTER. and smelling the buttery cabbage she couldn't help having a bite herself.

THE SERVING GIRL. This was an old habit of hers,

THE HUNTER'S MOTHER. and sure enough,

THE DAUGHTER. the same thing happened to her.

THE HUNTER'S FATHER. She couldn't hold the bowl with her new hooves,

THE HUNTER'S MOTHER. so she dropped it where it was and ran outside.

THE HUNTER'S FATHER. Meanwhile the witch's daughter was sitting talking to the messenger.

THE DAUGHTER. 'I don't know what's keeping them...
It does smell good.'

THE HUNTER'S MOTHER. The hunter thought that the magic must have happened by this time.

THE YOUNG HUNTER. 'Leave it to me. I'll go and get it.'

THE HUNTER'S FATHER. When he got to the kitchen

THE WITCH. he saw the two donkeys

THE SERVING GIRL. running around the courtyard,

THE HUNTER'S FATHER. and thought,

THE YOUNG HUNTER. 'Good! Just as I planned it, and serve them right.'

THE HUNTER'S MOTHER. He scooped up the cabbage that had fallen to the floor,

THE HUNTER'S FATHER. put it in the bowl

THE DAUGHTER. and brought it to the girl.

THE YOUNG HUNTER. She had some at once,

THE HUNTER'S MOTHER. and she too became a donkey

THE DAUGHTER. and ran outside.

THE HUNTER'S FATHER. The hunter washed his face

THE YOUNG HUNTER. so that they could recognise him,

THE HUNTER'S MOTHER. and went out to the courtyard with a length of rope.

THE YOUNG HUNTER. 'Yes, it was me. I've got you good and proper, and now you're going to pay for your treachery.'

THE HUNTER'S FATHER. He tied all three to the rope,

THE WITCH. and drove them ahead of him

THE SERVING GIRL. out of the castle

THE DAUGHTER. and along the road

THE YOUNG HUNTER. till they came to a mill.

THE SERVING GIRL. He knocked on the door. (*Knock, knock, knock.*)

THE MILLER. 'What d'you want?'

THE DAUGHTER. said the miller.

THE YOUNG HUNTER. 'I've got three ugly bad-tempered beasts here, and as they're no good to me I want to get rid of them. If you take them and treat them as I tell you, I'll pay whatever you ask.'

THE MILLER. That wasn't the sort of offer the miller got every day,

THE SERVING GIRL. so he agreed at once.

THE MILLER. 'How d'you want me to treat them, then?'

THE YOUNG HUNTER. 'Beat the old one three times a day, and feed her once'

THE WITCH. (that was the witch).

THE YOUNG HUNTER. 'The middle one can have three feeds a day and one beating'

THE SERVING GIRL. (that was the servant),

THE YOUNG HUNTER. 'and the young one's not too bad. Feed her three times and don't beat her at all.'

THE DAUGHTER. He couldn't bring himself to have the girl beaten.

THE YOUNG HUNTER. He went back to the castle and put his feet up.

THE WITCH. After a couple of days the miller came to see him.

THE MILLER. 'That old donkey, she wasn't much good. She's dead now. But the other two are looking really down in the mouth. I don't know what to do with them.'

THE YOUNG HUNTER. 'Oh, all right. I think they've probably been punished enough.'

THE SERVING GIRL. He told the miller to drive the other two donkeys back to the castle,

THE MILLER. where he spread some of the round cabbage leaves on the ground

THE YOUNG HUNTER. and let them eat,

The ghost of THE WITCH *watches forlornly, as the other two escape death.*

THE WITCH. so they became

THE DAUGHTER *and* THE SERVING GIRL. human beings again.

THE MILLER. The witch's beautiful daughter fell on her knees and said,

THE DAUGHTER. 'Oh, my dearest, forgive me for all the evil I did you! My mother forced me to do it. I never wanted to betray you, because I love you with all my heart. The wishing cloak is in the hall cupboard, and as for the bird's heart, I'll drink something to make me bring it up again.'

THE YOUNG HUNTER. 'No need for that,'

THE MILLER. he said,

THE WITCH. because he'd found himself in love with her all over again.

THE YOUNG HUNTER. 'You can keep it. It won't make any difference who has it, because I want to marry you.'

THE HUNTER'S MOTHER. Their wedding was celebrated soon afterwards,

THE DAUGHTER. and they lived together

THE YOUNG HUNTER. very happily

THE WITCH. until they died.

**Other Plays for Young People to Perform
from Nick Hern Books**

Adaptations

ANIMAL FARM
Ian Wooldridge
Adapted from George Orwell

ARABIAN NIGHTS
Dominic Cooke

AROUND THE WORLD IN 80 DAYS
Laura Eason
Adapted from Jules Verne

BAD GIRLS
Vicky Ireland
Adapted from Jacqueline Wilson

BEAUTY AND THE BEAST
Laurence Boswell

THE BOY IN THE STRIPED PYJAMAS
Angus Jackson
Adapted from John Boyne

CORAM BOY
Helen Edmundson
Adapted from Jamila Gavin

DAVID COPPERFIELD
Alastair Cording
Adapted from Charles Dickens

GREAT EXPECTATIONS
Nick Ormerod and Declan Donnellan
Adapted from Charles Dickens

HIS DARK MATERIALS
Nicholas Wright
Adapted from Philip Pullman

THE JUNGLE BOOK
Stuart Paterson
Adapted from Rudyard Kipling

KENSUKE'S KINGDOM
Stuart Paterson
Adapted from Michael Morpurgo